YOUNG MILLSY

My Autobiography

Gary Mills

First Edition.
First published 2021

Published by:
Morgan Lawrence Publishing Services Limited
71-75 Shelton Street
Covent Garden
London
WC2H 9JQ
www.morganlawrence.co.uk
email: info@morganlawrence.co.uk
Company number: 12910264

ISBN: 9781838232917

A CIP catalogue record is available from the British Library.

Photographs courtesy of: John Sumpter, Dave Morcom/*The Fox*,
The Northern Echo, York City FC, PA Images/Alamy Stock Photo,
Charlie Waugh, Martin Avery, Jeff Pruss, Leicester City FC

Cover design by LCGraphix.
Cover photograph courtesy of PA Images/Alamy Stock Photo

Typesetting by Mathew Mann
Proofreading by Amy Memory

Printed and bound in Bulgaria by Pulsio Print.

Bibliography

Acton, William, Prostitution, considered in its moral, social and sanitary aspects in London and other large cities. London, 1857.

Glover, James M., Jimmy Glover: His Book. London, 1911.

— Jimmy Glover and His Friends. London, 1913.

Hibbert, H. G., Fifty Years of a Londoner's Life. London, 1916.

—A Playgoer's Memories. London, 1920.

Hicks, Seymour, Between Ourselves. London, 1930.

Holden, W. H., They Startled Grandfather. Gay Ladies and Merry Mashers of Victorian Times. London, 1950.

Hollingshead, John, Gaiety Chronicles. London, 1898.

Jupp, James, The Gaiety Stage Door: Thirty Years' Reminiscences of the Theatre. London, 1923.

Macqueen-Pope, W., Gaiety: Theatre of Enchantment. London, 1949.

McKenna, Neil, Fanny and Stella: The Young Men Who Shocked Victorian England. London, 2013.

Marcus, Steven, The Other Victorians. London, 1966.

Mayhew, Henry, London Labour and the London Poor. London, Vols. I-III, 1851, Vol. IV, 1861.

Millward, Jessie, Myself and Others. London, 1923.

Moser, Maurice, and Charles F. Rideal, Stories From Scotland Yard. London, 1890.

—True Detective Stories. New York, 1891.

Nead, Lynda, Victorian Babylon. London, 2000.

Nicholson, Renton, The Lord Chief Baron Nicholson. An Autobiography. London, [1860].

Pearl, Cyril, The Girl with the Swansdown Seat. London, 1955.

—Victorian Patchwork. London, 1972.

Richie, J. Ewing, The Night Side of London. London, 2nd revised edn., 1858

Rowell, George, William Terriss and Richard Prince: Two Characters in an Adelphi Melodrama. London, 1985.

Scott, Clement, The Drama of Yesterday and To-day. London, 1899.

Sims, George R. My Life: Sixty Years' Recollections of Bohemian London. London, 1917.

Speaight, George, Bawdy Songs of the Early Music Hall. London, 1975.

Spehr, Paul, The Man Who Made Movies: W.K.L. Dickson. New Barnett, Herts., 2008.

Yates, Edmund, Edmund Yates: His Recollections and Experiences. London, 1885.

DEDICATED to everyone in my family for their support over the years in my football career.

Especially:

My beautiful wife Sue

My beautiful children; Ryan, Jenna and Ria

Mum and Dad; Jean and Roly

My sister and brothers; Angela, Martyn and Graham

Nan and Pap Frost; Kath and Tom

Pap Mills, Walter

Nan Mills, Bertha

I LOVE YOU ALL

Contents

MESSAGES FROM OUR SPONSORS

By RICHARD WARING, Nottingham Forest fan and director of Waring Engineering Limited. Proud sponsor of this book.

I FIRST saw Gary Mills as a teenager watching Brian Clough and Peter Taylor's great Forest side from the terraces and couldn't believe he was a year younger than me.

Like many other Forest fans, I don't think Gary and the rest of that small, but great, squad ever got the recognition they truly deserved, I have to pinch myself now thinking about all the great things they achieved.

Luckily, I once met the great man Brian Clough. I had an England shirt on which he had written 'I should have managed these buggers' and had signed it. I asked him if he would write and sign it to 'TOM DICK and HARRY' after me and my two sons. He told me jokingly to 'f--- off' then proceeded to write: 'TOM and HARRY, be good Brian'.

When the first European cup final came around, I was gutted as I had booked a holiday to Tenerife and couldn't make it. But I said to my mates, 'don't worry about it I will go to the next one' (can't believe I said that). I actually did go to the next European final which Gary played in when he took the place of the injured Trevor Francis. It was a bit like the Alamo, but all the lads played out of their skins, and we kept a clean sheet with the great Robbo scoring the winner.

In more recent years, I have been lucky enough to have met my Forest heroes socially and got to know Gary and the rest of the lads. They are truly down to earth people and very humble.

My wife Jayne and I have run a small family engineering company for nearly 30 years which employs around 12 staff. We manufacture repair sleeves and tees for gas and oil pipelines.

Over the years, I have sponsored in excess of 50 games at the City Ground inviting many of the European lads. I have used many of these games to promote a brilliant charity Jayne and I support - Blesma, the British limbless ex-service men and women's association, who support all their members from the age of 16 upwards for life. Gary's wife, Sue, actually ran the London marathon in aid of Blesma and raised valuable funds.

Gary Mills, along with other Forest greats; Jeff Whitefoot, Ian Storey-Moore, Kenny Burns John Robertson, Garry Birtles, Colin Barrett, John O'Hare, Liam O'Kane, Alan Hill, Ian Bowyer, and Peter Grummitt, have been my guests to watch the Epsom Derby. We have made this an annual event, and I do my best to spoil them, and we have a fantastic day out. I could not do this without the help from another great friend, Mike West, who pulls everything together.

I have got to know Gary very well over the years and have the great pleasure of calling him a good friend. When I was asked if it would be possible to sponsor his book, I said it would be a pleasure, I hope Young Millsy brings out the full story of a young man who I discovered was not only a talented footballer, but also outstanding at rugby and athletics.

Please enjoy the book!

By Jamie HEMMINGS, of Superstar Speakers. Proud sponsors of this book.

CELEBRITY events leaders Superstar Speakers are delighted to give their wholehearted and generous support to Young Millsy.

The Mansfield-based international company has flourishing links with many football legends including Nottingham Forest's European Cup winning side.

"Gary Mills is one of the famous players who has signed memorabilia in which we specialised even more after the lockdown of speakers' events," explained founder Jamie Hemmings.

"He is also expected to be involved in our programme of live events later this year."

"Therefore, when we were asked to sponsor Gary's autobiography, we were very pleased to do so, and we wish him every success."

The roots of this innovative business came in the midst of personal tragedy when Jamie, and his wife and co-founder Laura, lost a close friend back in 2011.

Former England footballer Neil 'Razor' Ruddock hosted a successful fundraising evening and the country's most capped player Peter Shilton took centre stage for the first 'business event'.

The biggest of names have followed including Paul Gascoigne, Roy Keane, and Eric Cantona.

Recent 'signings' now exclusive to Superstar Speakers include Stan Collymore and Wes Morgan. Sam Curran, arguably England's most exciting young Test cricket star, has Superstar Speakers as his bat sponsor.

Manchester United, Liverpool, Everton, Spurs, and Leeds legends are also on board.

"It's been an extremely frustrating time for us during lockdown," said Laura. "But we now have a very exciting line up of live events to look forward to."

For more information about Superstar Speakers, sponsors of Young Millsy, please go to superstarspeakers.co.uk.

Foreword by Garry Birtles, former Nottingham Forest striker

I REMEMBER, as if it happened yesterday, young Mills by the corner flag training with the first team and Lloydy (Larry Lloyd) kicking him up in the air. It was the big man's way of seeing if he could handle it and I stuck up for Gary.

Perhaps our friendship started because we were two young men thrust into the Forest team that day against Arsenal, one of the best teams in the land. I was 20 years old and Gary was just 16. Brian Clough and Peter Taylor didn't pick him because he was the teacher's pet – they would never put anyone in that position unless they could handle it.

The European Cup final in Madrid was the first time we ever played up front together. After a few minutes, Clough and Taylor saw we were getting battered and dropped Millsy back into midfield where he did a good job. Hamburg were the best team in Europe and we were massive underdogs. I was the first line of defence up front and Millsy and the midfield were next in line. We knew if we could nick a goal, we would be difficult to beat and that's what happened.

It's staggering now to think back on what we won at Forest and it was great that Gaz was a part of that.

We should also remember how good he was at Leicester City. He seemed to get better and better as the years went on and was part of that very close-knit team Brian Little put together. They seemed to get to Wembley every year in the play offs and I'm surprised Leicester let him go when they finally got to the Premier League.

I enjoyed playing in the same Notts County side with him after he signed for John Barnwell. With players such as Geoff

Pike, Paul Hart and Charlie McParland, we didn't think we'd be in the Third Division for long, but it wasn't to be.

Gary helped me by playing for Gresley during my short time in management and I think he has been a bit unlucky as a boss himself. I'm thinking particularly about his spell at Notts County and not just saying that as a mate.

The pressure was on us because we played under Clough, but every manager has to put his stamp on it and I think Gary did that. It staggers me to see managers continually getting the sack yet staying on the merry-go-round whilst others, like Gary, don't get a big break.

I know, for example, he did a really good job at Gateshead, but it isn't easy at Non-League level. Managers are beholden to owners and can so easily be left in limbo.

As a person, Gary is one of the nice guys in football. I used to go on holiday with him and Sue. I like the quote 'friends are like stars – you don't always see them, but you know they are there'. There's not a bad bone in his body and you can't help but be charmed by him. To make things worse, he's always been a good-looking bastard!

Introduction by Gary Mills

EUPHORIA! There is no other word for it. The split second the final whistle went, I flew off the bench and back onto the Bernabeu pitch to hug as many of my Nottingham Forest teammates as I could get hold of. In moments like that you have no idea what you are doing. It is like when scoring a goal, your head explodes, and you go into another world.

Now more than four decades on, I realise that none of us had any real idea what we had achieved that memorable Spanish night. I am not exaggerating when I say that being a part of Forest's double European Cup triumph means much more to me now in 2021 than it did then.

To think I was 18 years old – four years out of junior football – and played my part on football's ultimate club stage. 'From Long Buckby to the Bernabeu' as a relative said when considering a title for this book. Wow, just wow.

I don't mind admitting that last year there were tears in my eyes watching a TV programme on how Forest conquered Europe. It brought home once again the fact I played for that great Forest team and for Brian Clough, the 'Gaffer' as I call him, arguably the greatest manager. Call me biased but, in my view, that was the best achievement ever by any club team.

I ran a marathon on the pitch for 68 minutes in the 1980 European Cup final, starting up front and then dropping back into midfield as we fought for our lives against German side Hamburg. Fitness and adrenaline meant I wasn't tired when the Gaffer told me 'well done, son' and invited me to sit next to him on the substitutes' bench. The next 22 minutes, plus injury time, were far more nerve racking as I watched my mates resist wave after wave of Hamburg attacks.

We didn't just win that spring night. The physical and mental challenges that go into lifting that famous trophy are enormous. That triumph was the result of two years of glory in Amsterdam, Berlin, Zurich and bleakest Romania – not to mention Liverpool, the European champions we conquered, and what the boys achieved up and down England winning the First Division before I broke into the team.

As for me, that 'well done' could not have happened without my wonderful family, who gave me the perfect start in life and have supported me ever since, and the brilliant staff at Forest, who made a 14-year-old feel at home in the company of top-class professionals. Through this book, I'm saying my 'thank you' to all of you.

My story is not all about Forest. Two years later I played in a Soccer Bowl final in America, sandwiched by a brief period at Derby County, then back home I developed a new love affair with Leicester City, where I spent five unforgettable years. Notts County are another club I have a lot of affection for as I had two memorable spells there, both as a player and managing the club.

When I thought my body had given up on me, I went into management and have ridden the rollercoaster of successes and gutting failures. Mostly successes.

In Non-League football I have learnt much about the game I love. My headline story may be Nottingham Forest, but I value the fantastic people I have met on and off the pitch in the former Conference and lower leagues with just as much affection.

Whilst I would have loved to have managed at the very top, that winning feeling of a job 'well done' is the same whether the three points are gained at Liverpool or Arnold Town. I got that feeling all too briefly as manager of Southern League Corby Town in 2020/21 until our season was locked down and I look forward to experiencing it again in 2021/22.

At my side for 38 years has been my wonderful wife Sue. She knows more than anyone the sacrifices I have made and still make to pursue my interest in a game I was first introduced to by my Dad and Pap.

I hope you enjoy my story and enjoy your football.

CHAPTER 1
Family and the all-round sportsman

By DAVID POPE, sports teacher and assistant headteacher Campion School.

THE first thing I noticed about young Gary Mills was his amazing physique – and his ability as an all-round sportsman matched it. He was picked for all school sports teams - football, rugby, athletics, cross country and cricket all included.

The school sent a bus load to watch him be man of the match for England's rugby schoolboys against Portugal at Twickenham. Shortly afterwards we were at Wembley to see him play football for England. But, despite his level of achievement, Gary was never big headed or arrogant.

Typical of Gary was what happened one Saturday when his football match for Forest Reserves was called off. He came to the school for the rugby match, bringing his kit in case one of the players got injured. Then he volunteered to run the touchline for the whole game.

He was one of the first to return to school to present our sports awards and said how playing rugby developed his teamwork and discipline. Gary was a natural full back with phenomenal pace that made him one of the fastest sprinters in the country. But he realised that he could only do his job if his teammates did theirs. He also learnt not to argue with referees.

There's no doubt in my mind that he could have gone all the way in rugby – he was that good. I'm not a football man but his achievement in winning European Cups with Brian Clough's team was awesome.

*****

MY childhood was fantastic. I have nothing but happy memories of living in Harpole, a beautiful village on the outskirts of Northampton.

Dad Roland, known to all as Roly, had been a professional footballer. He spent his whole career with Northampton Town, making more than 300 appearances. But my first memories of him were working on the coaching staff and commercial side at The Cobblers, as he retired from playing when I was very young. I enjoyed going out with him as he brought in much-needed cash by selling lottery tickets and scratchcards in pubs and clubs. People often told me Roly was a 'good player'. That made a young son very proud.

Mum still lives in the same family house I was brought up in. She was a pub manager at The Paddocks in the village, working every hour God sent. Mike and Bernie Winters and The New Seekers were among those who performed in the cabaret room at the back.

Because Mum was so busy, I was always asking to stay with Nan and Pap, my Mum's parents. We lived in Garners Way and they were on Carrs Way near the green. Tom and Kath were very, very important to me and I loved them dearly. My Dad's dad Walter lived in Daventry and was a lovely man, but circumstances meant I saw less of him.

I was the middle boy of three – literally. We all slept in the same room with Martyn having a bed on one side and my younger brother Graham on the other. My sister Angela, sports mad and the eldest child, had a room to herself. Another special person in all our lives was Pat, who looked after us many times calling me in from the field for my tomato ketchup sandwiches.

I played outside as much as I could. There were no worries in those days. When I was around seven to nine years old, I walked down the alleyway with friends to the sports field to play on the field used by Harpole FC and the village cricket club. Then it was home for a snack before going back to the field where we carried on playing.

Saturday became my favourite day when Dad started taking me to Northampton Town. We went to a sweet shop on the corner next to the ground to get chocolate sweets with hundreds and thousands. Even now, I'm a big fan of sweets and can't usually resist buying them from the petrol station!

There were only three stands and sometimes the ball needed to be retrieved from the cricket pitch. Sadly, I missed the club's glory days when they went through the football leagues from 1960-61 to 1965-66 with Dad as the wing half. When he retired, he was in the top ten appearances for Northampton. With Dad still being part of the club, we always felt very welcome.

The most memorable Saturday of all at Northampton was on February 7 1970 as the Cobblers played mighty Manchester United in the FA Cup.

Around 22,000 fans crammed into the small ground, including Dad and I in the wooden main stand and my older brother Martyn in the aisle. There was no bigger football club than United and no footballer with a higher profile than George Best. The Irishman though had been having his problems. He had been suspended for four weeks for kicking a ball out of the referee's hands and, with United winning, there was even talk that they didn't need him.

This was the afternoon that he made history and changed my football life forever. I watched, mesmerised, as this genius scored six goals in an 8-2 United win. He showed any doubters how wrong they were by turning in a performance of a lifetime.

I wanted to be like George Best, to go past defenders and score bags of goals. I didn't become a United fan, but wanted to emulate Best's genius, from his mannerisms to his brilliant football. My parents saved up until we walked into Benny Collins' sports shop at the top of Gold Street for me to pick up my George Best kit – complete with shirt, shorts and socks.

The following year I turned on the TV at 9am for the FA Cup final between Arsenal and Liverpool. Final day was Christmas and birthday all rolled into one for me. There was *It's a Knockout*, interviews with players from both teams on the coaches on their way to Wembley and footage from recent games. Then we all sang ABIDE WITH ME and shed a few tears before the whole family sat down for the game itself. Highlight for me was the winning goal, a cracking shot from outside the box by Arsenal's Charlie George who then laid on his back with his arms in the air. From that day on, I was an Arsenal fan and wanted to be like Charlie George!

I already had a fair idea I was a footballer. I dribbled past players like Bestie and, in some games, scored even more than he did, often celebrating like Charlie George. Nan sponsored me at 10p a goal and it cost her a pound from a single game. That was when a pound was worth something!

Football was in my blood. Sadly, I didn't have time to watch Northampton very often as I was very busy – playing for the school and banging in the goals on a Sunday. After Dad finished playing professionally, he turned out for the Harpole village team which I thought was fantastic. They kicked off at either 2.15pm or 2.30pm, a fact I reminded him of as he sat having a cigarette in his kit and boots watching the 2pm race at Kempton Park. Dad liked a flutter and I'm the same. But it was never a serious thing for either of us.

Then Dad put out his fag, ran down the alleyway and straight onto the field! Harpole were a good village team but one thing was missing – a junior side. That's before Martyn and I had a brainwave: 'let's start our own team in the village'. We were about 10 or 11 years old.

Filled with excitement, we spoke with Mum. She pointed out the practicalities such as we had no kit. A jumble sale on the front lawn was never going to be a big earner, but a steady stream of villagers dropped by to support it. Then we washed cars for 10p or 20p. The pennies added up and we bought a blue kit – a big moment for us.

Now there was only one thing missing – a name! Mum suggested having a word with Bert Starmer, who lived at the bottom of our street and was football mad. My parents insisted I addressed him as 'Mr Starmer' or I risked a clip around the ear for being cheeky. Mr Starmer came up with a novel name we liked straightaway and I'm proud to say Harpole Trueshots are still a junior football club in the village. In fact it is now run as a successful academy with a lot of help from my brother Graham – amazing for a small village.

We arranged our first ever game after a guy from Northampton visited the village. Off we went on the bus in our kits the following weekend to Dallington Park. When we got there, the playing field was fine, but where were the goalposts? Our opponents explained it was 'jumpers down'.

Harpole Trueshots were a big thing for the Mills brothers, with Martyn and I in the team and Graham the club mascot.

Soon we were playing Sunday League football and had the thrill of travelling to a nearby village to play a cup final under lights.

I was a right winger, like Bestie. I was quick and good enough to score a lot of goals and totally enjoyed every minute. When we didn't have a game, I went down on my own to the playing field, being dragged home by Mum when it was so late, we could barely see each other.

I suffered my first rejection when the Harpole Primary school team was announced – Martyn was in it, I wasn't. I told Mum I was better than some and she phoned the headmaster. He said only pupils in their last year at the school could be picked. That didn't help – I just wanted to play!

I was good enough to get the attention of South Northants as the school sent me down for a trial. This was where Pap came into his own. He really wanted to come and watch. Parents and grandparents weren't welcome, but he was insistent. We went by bus together to Daventry and I joined the rest of the trialists. When my name was called, Pap chirped up: "He's an absolute natural – he doesn't need to have a trial!" If only the ground could have swallowed me up, I was so embarrassed. But I knew he meant well, and it was also a lovely moment. No harm was done as I was selected for the regional side.

'Big school' is an important and scary moment in any young person's life. Luckily, Bugbrooke Campion comprehensive school was only four miles away and very sports friendly.

*****

By ALAN ROSE

I KNEW Gary as I was a friend of his dad Roly and then he played alongside my son Steven for South Northants Boys, who became Long Buckby's junior side.

Managing Long Buckby was the best five years of my football life and Gary was exceptional. One season he and Steven both scored more than 100 goals.

Although he got involved with Forest at an early age, Gary was always keen to play for us and was part of our massive achievement when we won the Umbro Cup, a nationwide competition for under 14s.

Together we enjoyed great times, losing less than ten per cent of our games. Gary was absolutely fantastic and the lads all mixed in together so well there were more arguments among the parents than them. Long Buckby and Gary were good for each other.

I watched him progress in football as a Forest season ticket holder. He had an exceptional career all the way through.

★★★★★

Playing for South Northants had a good spin off, as the father of one of the lads, Alan Rose, formed a junior team at Long Buckby to go alongside their senior side. He spoke with Dad and I was more than happy to play for them as well as Harpole. I started in the under 12s and my game flourished.

I really started banging in the goals and increasing my bank balance, again with Nan's help! I remember I'd pick a horse and was offered 10p per the odds if it won. I chose number five, a grey horse, at 10-1 and it won me another £1. Ever since I always choose the horse wearing five - not an infallible system, but it means something to me.

I was 13 years old when a Nottingham Forest scout approached me after playing for Long Buckby Juniors and invited me to the City Ground. Dad took his name and number. Thank you, Nick Turner, for having faith in me. I found out afterwards that he is from Corby and would still like to thank him in person if he is still around.

Then my parents taught me an invaluable lesson about loyalty, one that has stuck with me to this day. Harpole's top of the league rivals asked me to play for them. I casually began a conversation at the dinner table on the lines of 'by the way, Dad, I'm going to play for a top of the league team!', Mum and Dad weren't happy. I was ordered to put my knife and fork down, go upstairs, wait until they had finished their dinner, then come back down for a chat.

They were going to teach me something important. I had helped to form Harpole and was still playing football with my mates. It didn't matter a jot where Harpole or the other team was in the league, I should support my mates and not throw away all the hard work I put in. And that's what I did, sticking with my schedule of playing football twice a day on both Saturday and Sunday. I'm so grateful my parents not only supported me every inch of the way, but took the time and effort to put me right when they needed to.

Three other lads from Long Buckby went with me to the City Ground for trials which led to me signing schoolboy forms when I was 14. My friends weren't offered terms at Forest, but both signed for other clubs. I went to Forest during school half term and other convenient dates and forged a good relationship with them. One of those who helped me get established was Alan Hill, who held a variety of roles at Forest. Hilly, Liam O'Kane, and scout Brian Newton, all watched me play several times.

Forest weren't the only team interested. Northampton offered a trial – an emotional pull because of my Dad. I also went to Leicester City for a few days where I learnt a useful lesson. Back at our digs, after training at Belvoir Drive, one of the lads asked if I wanted a beer. I'd only ever drunk Nan's advocaat at Christmas and couldn't believe someone trying to get signed on schoolboy forms wanted alcohol! Not for me. . .

My introduction to Brian Clough was very memorable. Alan Hill sent a message to make sure I did well in a Sunday League game in the Derby area because the manager was coming to watch! That had almost slipped my mind when I was squealing in pain after being sent crashing by a tackle near the touchline. Looking up, I saw this man with a dog shouting 'f---ing get up!', I had no idea it was Brian Clough! Our trainer came on with his sponge and bucket only for this guy, wearing a cap and carrying a stick, to say: "There's nothing f---ing wrong with him. Get up, son, keep playing!". As he became more and more vocal, it dawned on me who he was. That wasn't the last time the Gaffer gave me that order!

Forest were the only club I was ever going to sign for, but that was nothing to do with Brian Clough. He was still new to the job at the City Ground and I honestly didn't know much about him. Being a mad keen Arsenal fan, I was more interested in Bertie Mee. Instead it was the kind support of Alan Hill and others, plus the fact I enjoyed my sessions there, that swung me towards Forest.

I told my parents Forest were pushing to sign me and was delighted they were made a fuss of when the big day arrived.

Forest were playing a home match at the City Ground and Alan Hill took me and my parents to Antonio's, an Italian restaurant on Trent Bridge, to begin the evening with a meal. Then we went to the City Ground where Clough said he was delighted I was signing schoolboy forms. He ordered a bottle of champagne with glasses for all four of us to toast the occasion. This time I couldn't refuse!

Clough surprised me by taking me down to the Forest dressing room where the team was getting ready for the match. There he introduced me to Terry Curran, a lightning-fast winger I liked watching, and told him: "Oi, you, do you know who this young man is?". When Terry shook his head, the manager went on: "Remember his name, Gary Mills, he is going to be taking your f----ing place, son. Remember his name." I understand Terry still remembers that as well as I do!

Afterwards Clough asked if I thought I could be 'a better player than Terry Curran'. I didn't know what to say, so said 'yes'. "Right, that's good to hear, son," the manager added.

Life became very hectic. I barely had a minute to myself, but it was a magical time. I was at Forest every moment I possibly could. Often Angela and her boyfriend Kelvin drove me from Northants in her Ford Escort. A fairly lengthy journey seemed to take forever in that rickety vehicle, but I will always be thankful. I love my sister to bits and still do – she always wanted to help me progress and become successful. In addition to Forest, I was playing for Long Buckby's senior team and Harpole and making waves in two other sports. All this on top of my schoolwork!

The school was very good to me, giving me time off to go to Forest when I needed to. I excelled at sport rather than my academic studies. Mum and Dad reminded me I needed options other than football, but I was always confident I would make it.

I was also a natural at both rugby and athletics. I went on to represent England Schoolboys at both football and rugby and finish the sixth fastest 100m sprinter in my age group in the All-England athletics championship. I partly credit my brother Martyn for how fast I could run. I did the 100m in 11 seconds and some of my quickest sprints were running away from my bro! I won't call him a bad loser, but he didn't like it. When I bowled him at cricket, he said it was a 'no ball'. Then I ran as fast as I could back home with Martyn chasing me stump in hand.

Forest were brilliant from the very start in making me feel at home with the Gaffer again surprising me. There were two training pitches – I was with the youth team and the first team were playing a practice match. Out of the blue, he said: "Oi, young man, come over here, son, and train with us!" He threw me a bib and at 14 years of age I was training with the Forest first team.

I was excited, not overawed, but Larry Lloyd soon gave me a message about the senior game. Having skinned him on the right wing, I tried to repeat it. This time he crunched in a tackle sending me spinning up into the air. When I landed, Lloydy was in my face shouting: "Do that again, I'll break your f---ing leg!" Garry Birtles, another of the younger players, rushed over and called Lloyd a 'f---ing disgrace'. Brian Clough said nothing. A useful lesson about the real football world!

Soon afterwards Forest asked the school's permission to play me in their Central League side. My debut was on a Wednesday evening with the school kindly giving me the day off. Dad travelled to Nottingham with me as we played Liverpool Reserves, including several household names I knew from *Match of the Day*. I was on the wing in direct competition with Joey Jones, a Welsh international and a hard man. I was nervous, but felt I did ok. Liam O'Kane was in charge, but the manager walked in at half time with the message: "You, son, next time you don't pass the f---ing ball and shoot, I will chop your balls off." Then he added: "Listen to me, son, you might as well learn at 14 as at 24." The Gaffer also reacted to a pass I played to Sean Haslegrave in the second half. "Unbelievable, son," he said.

That was the start of exciting times for me with Forest Reserves. Angela drove me to Nottingham to stay in the apprentices' digs on the Friday when we were playing away the following afternoon. Grounds we went to included Old Trafford where Manchester United fielded Brian Greenhoff, Gordon Hill and Sammy McIlroy, fantastic players I watched as a kid, and Maine Road, where Colin Bell, the well-known England international midfielder, was Manchester City's star man.

Those were magical days, and the way Brian Clough and co nurtured me and made me feel at home and part of things was top class. I felt wanted and confident and had a fair amount of success scoring a few goals playing as a right winger in the Gaffer'ss favourite 4-4-2. When Forest didn't have a game, I either played for Dad's Long Buckby senior or junior side. He knew I was mentally strong enough to put all other things to one side and do my best for him.

I thoroughly enjoyed school where I was ok academically whilst getting most of my fulfilment from sport, but this didn't go down well with everyone. After a football match between the teachers and the pupils, one of my teachers came up to me and said: "You aren't as good as you think you are." This was very strange and unnecessary and turned into a form of bullying.

He made more and more comments- giving me the feeling he was green-eyed about me playing for Forest Reserves and thought I was a big-time Charlie. He even grabbed me around the neck in class. I didn't say anything and fully understand why the bullied sometimes keep things to themselves. This didn't change my overall view of school in any way as I loved my time there and made some great friends including Nick Verity, who went on to play at Long Buckby with me and remains a great mate today.

My England Schoolboys journey started with Midlands trials at Stafford before the northern area trials, then the nationals. I was in the last 24, playing as a winger when one of the coaches told me: "I'd like you to play right back." I told him I wasn't a full back, but he insisted, and I went on to have the game of my young life. Then it dawned on me – I was 15 years old and had a good chance of being selected for England.

I was nervous waiting for that envelope to drop through the letterbox. Then one Saturday morning it happened! I knew this was the letter because ESFA (England Schools Football Association) was stamped on the front. They were pleased to tell me I'd been picked for the England schoolboys' team!

I have never seen prouder people than Mum and Dad, my brothers and sister. They were so pleased for me. There was one more very important person to tell. Harpole were playing over the field that day with Pap standing there with his walking stick.

"Hiya, Pap, I've got something to tell you," I said. "I have got into the England team!"

Pap broke down in tears. "I knew you could do it – I'm so proud of you!" I was so, so lucky nobody reacted with a hint of jealousy at my success. Family and friends were thrilled for me.

There was a big occasion for Long Buckby when we reached the national Umbro Junior Cup final against Sale Dynamo. Appropriately for me, the final was played at the City Ground and we won. We had an incredible junior side at Long Buckby –

to this day I still don't know how any of those lads didn't go on to become professionals. Alan Rose, the manager, was brilliant – we had professionalism in abundance in those five unforgettable years. Without doubt, they helped me go on to achieve what I did in football.

Altogether I played about eight times for England including against Scotland at Wembley and Edinburgh and Northern Ireland at Blackpool. When we faced Holland at Middlesbrough's Ayresome Park, Ruud Gullit was in the Dutch team, although I didn't know anything about him at the time. Similarly, we faced Ian Rush when we tackled Wales. West Germany at Wembley was broadcast live on ITV, another personal first.

The Scottish game at Wembley was most memorable as I scored my one and only England goal. I was playing right back, facing up to a young lad called Colin Walsh who was also on schoolboy forms at Forest. The goal was a total fluke, but that didn't matter. I floated a free kick a few yards into their half and into the penalty area, where it eluded everyone and finished up in the back of the net. We won 2-0 to cap a great day. A bus load travelled from school, and local teams supported me in person by travelling down from Northampton. There were several good luck telegrams when I went into the dressing room, including one from the Gaffer (Brian Clough).

My rugby talent became clear because that was the school's main sport, rather than football. Dad thought I was too busy with my football to play a sport he wrote off as 'all arse and whistle'. He argued his point strongly with Mr Pope, but I'm glad the teacher stood his ground. The school wanted me to play, so it was right that I did. It was never going to be my first choice, but rugby was another adventure during an incredible period of my life.

I was a full back and caught the eye of scouts as I was first selected for South Northants trials, then Northants, and onto the national trials held at an army barracks. Immediately I saw one of the differences between football and rugby. We slept in dormitories preparing for our big day as there was no money in rugby.

I was one of four lads from Northampton at the trials with brothers Matthew and John Ebsworth and Gary Leonard being the others. Things again went well for me and after the final trial I was selected to play for a second set of England Schoolboys.

Playing for my country against Portugal at Twickenham was special, scoring two tries was even better. I know former Ipswich and Leicester defender Russell Osman shares my honour of playing for England Schoolboys at both sports, but I think I'm the only one to score at both Wembley and Twickenham. Northampton Saints took an interest and wanted me to go for a trial, but it wasn't right for me. Even then I knew where I was going to end up.

A game in France provided me with another unforgettable occasion although not for all the obvious reasons. The match was very tight and low scoring. I think it was 5-5 going into the last minute of the game when I joined the line and received the ball. My speed was key as I got myself over the line to score the winning try. There was time for us to miss the conversion before the referee blew the final whistle to start our celebrations.

I felt a million dollars. The great feeling stayed with me as I showered and changed and the staff said they'd take us to a restaurant in the square for a meal. Rugby is renowned for its social side and we were singing and having a great time before taking part in a drinking game. We downed a few halves of lager and got a bit tipsy before the manager took us by surprise. He ordered us outside into the square, then to take off all our clothes – last one back had to drink half a lager straight down at the bar. One consolation – it was almost dark, but no getting away from the rules. We didn't have a stitch on between us!

Suddenly it was mayhem. Police were everywhere and we were in trouble. The manager told us to gather our clothes and race back to the hotel. I put on my top and pants, scooped the rest of my clothes in my arms and ran as fast as I had during the game. We were ticked off one by one as we rushed into the small hotel. Finally, we were safe – we had all made it back. I don't know what the bigger achievement was – winning the match or getting to the hotel without being arrested! Either way, we were representing our nation and having an incredible time. You can't put a price on memories. I loved it.

I don't know how far I could have gone in athletics. But there was no doubting my pace. I was a good sprinter, whilst in the cross-country races I built up an early lead, then found myself gradually overtaken. The real choice was between rugby and football. Rugby officials wanted me to pursue the sport, but my heart was set on Nottingham Forest.

CHAPTER 2
SWEET SIXTEEN AND
THE GAFFER

By Alan Hill, former assistant manager of Nottingham Forest.

BRIAN CLOUGH had me in his office the day after Millsy signed schoolboy forms for Forest. He had a bottle of champagne in his hand and congratulated me on making a great signing. Then he told me that was my job and to find him another one!

Gary Mills was wanted by almost every big club in the country at the age of 14. We had good links in Northamptonshire and Brian Oldham scouted him at Long Buckby. In his youth, he was a brilliant all-round sportsman, playing rugby as well as football for England Schoolboys and being one of the fastest runners in the country.

A smashing lad, from a really good family, it helped that his Dad was a former footballer and understood what Forest were all about. I invited Gary to the City Ground with his Mum and Dad on a night the first team were playing Bolton. I took them out for dinner and back to the ground where they met Brian. He told me to bring him down to the dressing room after he signed.

Gary needed no persuading, so I took him to see the Gaffer as the lads were preparing for the game. The boss introduced Gary to our young winger Terry Curran waving the forms in his face. "Thickbonce, can you read? This is Gary Mills and he will take your place in two years!"

Gary made his First Division debut just over two years later against Arsenal. He'd been training with the first team from the age of 14. He then went on to play in the European Cup final against Hamburg and did very well for us.

Gary was a lovely lad – the type you'd want your daughter to marry – and, as Brian Clough said, a great signing.

SIGNING as an apprentice at Forest in July 1978 at the age of 16 was a big turning point in my young life. It was also when I learnt how brutal the sport is. Lads turned up at the City Ground to be signed or let go. Called in one by one that inevitably meant more went home gutted than happy. It was very difficult seeing young people I had got to know in such a mess.

Some didn't know until that brief meeting whether their football dream was beginning or about to be blown apart. I was luckier. The club had made it clear where I stood. They nurtured and encouraged me from day one and introduced me to the first team.

What a club I was signing for! When I first went to the City Ground they were a modest Second Division side, now Forest were First Division champions and League Cup holders.

It had been a real thrill when Forest paid for me to travel to Old Trafford with my Dad to watch us tackle Liverpool in the League Cup final replay. I was on the train from Nottingham to Manchester with buoyant and excitable Forest fans getting ready for a very big occasion. They didn't have a clue who I was. Must have thought I was just another fan. I longed to tell them I played for Forest Reserves but kept quiet. That was the night when Phil Thompson fouled John O'Hare somewhere near the penalty area and John Robertson stroked the penalty past Ray Clemence to give us our first major trophy since winning the FA Cup before I was born in 1959. The fact Forest allowed me to join in that occasion meant a lot – again I was getting a first-hand insight into what it was really like to be a professional footballer.

Committing myself to Forest was the start of a new life and the end of another – a truly amazing and beautiful upbringing that gave me the perfect foundation for what lay ahead. Although very excited about taking a big step towards becoming a professional footballer, I cried my eyes out. It was a very, very emotional time. I was leaving home and a village I loved – people who meant so much to me.

I went to a restaurant with family and friends for a leaving do, feeling like the world was coming to an end. Both my brothers and Angela were emotional and so was I. But it was still a lovely evening. Next day Pap, bless him, gave me a little horseshoe for good luck that I've kept ever since. Leaving all that behind was heart-breaking. No other word does it justice.

Nan and Pap were so important in my life. They came with us to Butlins on our family holidays. We usually went to Bognor Regis. They were as excited when I won a prize at one of their sports events as when I achieved anything in football. Even if I have to say it a thousand times, my upbringing was fabulous. It played a massive, massive part in my life that made me the confident young man I became.

Now I was on my way to Nottingham. Alan Hill asked me to pop in and see him before I made my way to the digs, the same club premises I'd stayed at for the Central League games. Hilly, then landlord of The Rancliffe Arms at Bunny, told me he'd bet £100 on me playing for England at every level, including the seniors. That boosted my confidence. In the end I got a cap for every level, up to and including England Under 21s, but never a full international call up.

Dad took me to the NatWest Bank near Trent Bridge to open my first bank account before we went back to my digs where I stayed with Tom and Olive who looked after me and fellow apprentices. I showed Mum my bedroom and that was it. Mum and Dad said goodbye and my new life had begun. I was grown up and living on my own.

Like all football fans, I spent as much time as possible that summer watching the World Cup in Argentina. For the second tournament running England didn't make it to the finals. Scotland, including Forest's Kenny Burns, Archie Gemmill and John Robertson, got knocked out at the group stage, so my eyes were on the hosts. There were tickertape receptions, great players like Osvaldo Ardiles and Mario Kempes, and the perfect ending for Argentina as they beat Holland 3-1 to lift the World Cup.

Now a big occasion was on the horizon. Tottenham Hotspur, newly promoted to the First Division and having signed Ardiles and fellow World Cup winner Ricky Villa, were at the City Ground on the opening day of the 1978/9 season. I watched as the Spurs coach arrived and their kit was brought into the ground. I looked at Ardiles' boots, touching the leather, feeling the softest boots in the world. That was as near as I expected to get to first team football. The match finished 1-1 with Villa scoring for Spurs as Forest started with a series of draws.

I was staying with Colin Walsh and Don McCloud among others in the club's digs and my working day started at 8.30am. As an apprentice, I cleaned the boots of Kenny Burns and Peter Shilton. The rota was laid out for us. Training kits needed to be got ready for the morning, then I trained with the first team whilst preparing for the next Central League game.

The first team weren't quite firing, not scoring a goal for four games, but nothing prepared me for what happened next. The visit of Arsenal, the club I idolised for years, made September 9 1978 special for me. I never dreamt I'd be playing!

The way it happened was this. Every Friday the first team players went into the boardroom where the Gaffer read out the team for the weekend. Liam O'Kane said the boss wanted me there and, when I walked in, Brian Clough was already at the door. I later realised this wasn't usual. Often he kept the players waiting for a full hour. Did he get there on time to make me feel more settled? I'll never know . . .

"Alright, son, you can get me a beer and, while you're at it, get yourself one." he said.

"I don't drink, boss," I replied.

"You do now!" Clough said, "You will have a Guinness and you'll have it with me and ask all the other lads what they want."

I did as the boss said, grabbed myself a bottle of Guinness and sat down. Peter Taylor, typically, cracked a few jokes to relax us before the manager read out the side. "Shilton, Anderson, Clark, McGovern, Lloyd, Burns, MILLS . . ." Did he just say that? John Robertson, sitting next to me, confirmed I heard right. I was making my First Division debut against Arsenal at the age of 16!

The team was dismissed with a 'see you tomorrow' and I sat deep in thought. I wanted Mum and Dad, Nan and Pap and everyone to know straightaway. Trainer Jimmy Gordon said: "Right, son, I'll pick you up at 10am to watch the youth team." That, I think, was another way Clough ensured I didn't get too nervous. Jimmy continued: "Get on the phone. Let your Mum and Dad know. Find out how many tickets you want and tell Paul White (Forest assistant secretary)." My family were happy, if bewildered.

The lads immediately welcomed me into the fold. I was invited to Mackays café, at the back of the cricket ground, our usual place to unwind after the Friday meeting. We drunk tea and had a sausage or bacon cob – or even both. Being invited there meant I already felt a part of things. The other apprentices at the digs were confused why I was allowed nine match tickets when they only had two. I told them I was in the team!

After watching the youth game, I joined the rest of the lads in West Bridgford for our usual pre-match meal of steak and toast. There was time for a game of 'killer' on the snooker table before catching a lift to the City Ground. Before l knew it, I was running out to play against Arsenal!

You couldn't make this up. Of all teams to make my debut against, it had to be the Gunners! Had I written it myself, I'd have been laughed at for being corny. I was on the right side of midfield with Garry Birtles, making his First Division debut up front.

As we lined up for kick off, the nearest player was Arsenal's Graham Rix, beginning to establish himself at international level. "Good luck," he said, giving me a thumbs up. What a very nice gesture.

I thought I did alright. I went past full back Sammy Nelson two or three times as we gradually turned the game around after Liam Brady gave the Gunners an early lead. We were on our way to a 2-1 win with goals from Robbo and Ian 'Bomber' Bowyer when I went down with cramp with a few minutes left. Of all places, it was bang in front of the Forest dug out. "F---ing get up," cried the manager. I'd heard that somewhere before! I struggled like mad to get to my feet, but Jimmy had to give me a piggyback off the field – what a picture that was!

Two years of nurturing prepared me for that day. I didn't feel like a little boy going into a massive day. Good people had shown they believed in me and I had a good head on my shoulders. Among those to congratulate me on my debut was school friend Kenny Vincelete, who phoned next day to say how proud he was of me. We had parted company at school as recently as the summer and when he heard I was playing for Forest he hopped onto a train from Northampton, bought himself a match ticket and watched me from the terraces. I appreciated that very much.

Immediately after the game, my mind was on the Wednesday as Forest had a huge occasion in the first round of the European Cup. There were mixed feelings when we drew Liverpool of all teams – reigning champions of Europe and now our fierce domestic rivals. It was another surreal occasion to be part of, even though I didn't get on the pitch in either leg.

Just looking at the Liverpool players in the programme brought home how quickly my life was moving. When Emlyn Hughes, the former England captain, attended a function at The Paddocks, where Mum worked, with Duncan McKenzie, I never dreamt of being in competition with him in the European Cup. Graeme Souness and Kenny Dalglish were huge international stars, Steve Heighway was a fellow winger I watched with a lot of interest and Phil Neal had been coached by Dad at Northampton.

I was more than pleased being named among the five substitutes, with the Gaffer opting to play Archie Gemmill wide on the right. I sat on the bench that exciting and memorable night wondering 'what on earth is happening to me?' I was being treated in much the same way as established Forest stars Peter Shilton, Viv Anderson, and John Robertson.

My mate Gaz Birtles got his first professional goal and full back Colin Barrett blasted a cracking second just before the final whistle. Garry recalls how he was taunted by Liverpool's Phil Thompson asking if one goal would be enough. Gaz beat Thompson near the byline when Barrett made it 2-0 before saying: "Will two be enough, Phil?"

It was another thrill going to Anfield for the return game when I was again on the bench. Most of the country was convinced Liverpool would overturn our lead, but that was one of Forest's best defensive performances as we limited Liverpool to half chances and earned a 0-0 draw.

That meant we were going to Europe for real and the boss made it extra special with the way he treated me. I never knew what was coming next when I was told the Gaffer wanted me in his office, but this time he said: "Young man, I would like your Mum and Dad to come to Athens. Do you think they would come?"

"How would they get there? I asked.

"They will come on the f---ing plane with us, it's too far to f---ing walk, son" he said.

I couldn't wait to ask. It was exciting to be involved myself, brilliant my parents were made to feel part of what was happening to me and Forest. There was a party atmosphere on the plane with the players taking turns in the cockpit before settling back into their seats for the descent.

We stayed in a hotel built into a rock and again I got a message to see the Gaffer the day before the game. Sitting on his hotel room balcony overlooking the sea, we had one of our friendliest conversations. He insisted I had a beer and asked how my parents were enjoying being there. "I think you are a lovely young man," he said, before asking how I thought I had done in the first team so far. I thought I had done alright, and he added: "I think you have done extremely well!" He then asked which position I considered to be my best and even said I was the type of young man he would be happy to see his daughter with. I never thought of that as man management at the time, but it most certainly was. He made me feel ten feet tall.

Again I was an unused substitute as Forest walked out into an atmosphere unlike anything back home. We had stuff thrown at us and flares going off in the stands. It was very volatile and a test of our mental strength which we passed with flying colours by winning 2-1 despite the referee awarding Athens a joke penalty in the second half.

The return game gave me my chance to contribute to Forest's first European Cup win when I came off the bench at the City Ground. Left back Frank Clark was injured just before half time with us already leading 3-0 on the night when the manager said I was on. Whether the Gaffer would have given me the nod had the tie been in the balance, I don't know. I would like to think so. But it was a good experience for me all round as I enjoyed the second half and two more goals from Gaz Birtles helped us to a 5-1 victory.

That appearance at the age of 16 makes me still the youngest player and winner of the European Cup. Appropriately, perhaps, I was on a grand wage of £16 a week.

CHAPTER 3
TWO EUROPEAN CUPS, ONE MEDAL

MY NEXT big day almost put Arsenal in the shade. It was November 11 1978, my 17th birthday, and I signed professional forms for Forest. My brother Martyn, a big football fan, witnessed the special occasion and got a typical introduction to the Gaffer. "Get your hands out of your pockets!" he told him as we walked into the office with Mum and Dad.

Soon things were moving even faster in my new world as, with the ink still drying on my contract, I was in the starting line-up for the return match with Spurs and, yes, that man Ardiles.

There were 57,000 fans in a bristling White Hart Lane. But Clough pulled off a masterful piece of psychology to raise my confidence. The Gaffer told his mate Brian Moore, the ITV commentator: "Brian, can I introduce you to this young man? He is Gary Mills, and he is going to take the piss out of Perryman and Ardiles."

Take the piss out of him? I watched in awe as he lifted the World Cup and was proud picking up his boots. Yet that's what happened. I was in direct competition with the Argentinian maestro in the middle of the park and had an unbelievable game as Ardiles was subbed! We won 3-1 and Jimmy Gordon came onto the pitch, not to carry me off this time, but to congratulate me on my performance. I could hardly believe it myself.

Domestically, I was on the move. Colin Walsh, Don McCleod and I switched digs to Gedling where Mrs Osborne was our landlady. This gave us some independence. I was the odd one out not being Scottish, but we got on very well. We caught the bus to the City Ground together for training and Mrs Osborne looked after us by doing our cooking and washing - basically everything.

A lovely lady who had lost her husband, she treated us all like we were family. We were there for about a year.

Getting used to Brian Clough's ways was a culture shock. The stories of heavy drinking by the manager and the team were just that – stories. But alcohol was a factor. There was a two-litre bottle of whiskey in the dressing room which we took with us on away trips. The Gaffer asked if the lads wanted a drink just before going onto the field. Some took a swig to keep warm and calm nerves.

I spent a fair amount of time in my first two seasons on the bench waiting for the Gaffer to say: "Son, get warmed up, you're going on". Although part of the team, the manager kept my feet on the ground by making me clean boots and mop down the dressing room. I also combined being involved with the first team with playing for the reserve and youth teams.

We all knew our jobs very well. There was never much talk, if any, about the opposition, we were simply told to go out and play. I was encouraged to take on the full back, get to the byline and pick someone out, if I could. Fans sometimes accused Brian Clough's team of 'trying to walk the ball in', but his tactics made sense. Rather than take a pot shot at goal, he told us to get our heads up and pick out a player with a better chance.

Jimmy Gordon paid me the compliment of being 'the best crosser of a ball I have ever seen', and even brought a friend with him to watch me play in a reserve game at the Baseball Ground. I had to apologise to Jimmy afterwards for putting a couple of crosses behind the goal.

My two closest friends in the Forest squad were Bryn Gunn and Gaz Birtles. It was Liam O'Kane who introduced me to Gunny, perhaps because he was also from Northamptonshire. He said Gunny would look after me and he didn't let me down. I always found him to be loyal, and a great bloke. When I moved into different digs in Stapleford with Walshy and Don in January 1980, Gunny lived nearby.

In my opinion, people underestimate the role Gunny played at Forest. He was a true club man for years and never fully appreciated. It was always the way for some reason. The Heanor branch of the supporters' club held a dinner on a Saturday evening with three Forest guests – Gunny, Colin Walsh, and me. We were sat behind the stage as the host announced us one by one. Walshy was the first to walk on to loud applause and I was next. Then he announced the third and final guest 'Ben Green'. We still laugh about that when we get together. It could only have happened to Gunny.

I had a link with Gaz Birtles because I made my debut on the same day he came back into the side against Arsenal. We became very good friends, later holidaying together with our families.

The Gaffer liked to room me with Forest captain John McGovern on trips. John was one of the more experienced players and always helpful towards me. I think the Gaffer wanted me to learn from a great professional. He ran, rather than walked, back to the ground after training on Trentside and encouraged me to run with him. John was a very good captain at Forest. Rooming together also worked well because we were both very good sleepers. Often we had three hours sleep in the afternoon before a game and both slept soundly. He taught me a lot about how to prepare for a game. This was another way in which the Gaffer disciplined me to do the job.

All the group were great with me and didn't talk down to me because I was the youngest. I didn't socialise with a lot of them, but when we went out as a group – which was often – I was always included. We socialised and had a few beers together, something missing in the modern game. I felt privileged to be with them even when I wasn't old enough to drink. Some might think socialising together wouldn't help us on the pitch. But the opposite was true - it helped foster team spirit.

Only the occasional new player came into the squad. Largely it was the same group who knew each other so well. This gave us such a strength of unity. The attitude was 'if it isn't broke, don't fix it' and signings were made only when we needed them. Our squad only included sixteen players: eleven starters, a substitute and four who usually played a reserve game on the same day. Clough and Taylor never spent big cash on new signings when a youngster was coming through. That's how lads like myself and Gaz got our chance when they could have looked elsewhere. Team spirit is vital in any workplace. When a new player didn't integrate or was a bit aloof, they didn't tend to be with us for long because the Gaffer knew the importance of being a team. In the same way when he suggested a social meeting himself, all of us went out.

Quite often after a game on the Saturday, the Gaffer said: "See you on Thursday!" I remember sitting on the bus after losing an away match when the Gaffer said to John McGovern: "Captain, when do you think we should come in, son?"

John, being a fitness fanatic and a keen trainer, said: "Monday".

The boss said: "See you Thursday, lads."

Liam O'Kane argued 'that's ridiculous' only for Clough to say: "I will make the decisions, Liam." There was then whispering between Liam and a few lads who wanted to come in for a secret training session earlier in the week. So rather than making excuses to skip training, our lads sometimes went against the rules to train more!

Some came in and did an hour's training. There were also times when Shilts wanted to do a bit more. With no such thing as a goalkeeping coach, I was one of the players who went to the training ground with him to keep him happy with some afternoon drills. Spending so little time training had its problems. What could we do to fill the rest of the day? I wasn't into two of the most popular pursuits – golf and betting – but did go down the pub with the lads.

If they saw Premier Division footballers out having a drink, supporters would almost certainly tell the club and think the players weren't working hard enough. But those times were lovely. We bumped into fans and had a good chat with none of those worries. The Jubilee Club after the game was another place we met supporters: win, lose, or draw.

On a Monday or Tuesday when there was no midweek game, we often met in a bar called Uriah Heap, opposite Paul Smith's original shop, at about 1.30pm. That was better than training and going back to our digs alone.

I was in Forest's 'A' or third team when Trevor Francis, Britain's first ever million-pound player, made his debut in front of a handful of spectators on a park pitch on a Saturday morning. The Gaffer arrived after about 15 minutes and stopped the game! "Excuse me, referee," he said, "One of the players in my team isn't wearing shin pads." It was Trevor, who said he didn't possess any. So, the Gaffer ensured the game was stopped whilst some shin pads were brought out for him.

I scored my first Football League goal in an important game against Leeds at Elland Road in May 1979 in a performance that had the media speculating whether I would start in the European Cup final. The Gaffer's words before the game shocked me. I hadn't taken in the story of his fall out with Leeds where he was sacked after just 44 days, so his venom took me by surprise when he said: "We've got to beat this cheating lot."

My big moment came in the first half as we opened the scoring. Robbo got to the byline and his cross eluded a couple of Leeds defenders. The opposite winger was always told to get to the back post and I was there to stab the ball into the net from about five yards. The feeling was unbelievable, like nothing on earth. I had scored in an important game for Forest at the age of 17.

Sadly, I left Elland Road with an entirely different memory after a disgusting incident after we had won 2-1. A young woman, probably in her 20s, came onto the pitch and spat straight into my face. I gather the Gaffer was furious when I told him in the dressing room and wanted to involve the police, but there was nothing they could do.

Three nights later we went to The Hawthorns needing to beat West Brom to overhaul them and finish runners up. I was an unused sub as Trevor Francis scored a late winner in our last major game before the European Cup final against Malmo. I say 'major' but you should have seen the side the manager fielded just seven days before the final against Notts County in the County Cup. It was probably our strongest available line up.

Although I knew I had done well against Leeds in particular, I had no idea whether I'd be in the team in Munich. I was included in the youth team tour of Switzerland but told to travel to Germany to join up with the first team on the Monday before the European Cup final on the Wednesday night. The scenes in Munich were unbelievable with thousands of people from Nottingham in the city to cheer us on.

My big moment came after we trained on the morning of the final. Back at the hotel, Brian Clough read out the team and there was disappointment for a couple of big names. The Gaffer had specifically told the injured Archie Gemmill to get himself fit and he would start. But, although he and Martin O'Neill told the boss they were ok, both were named as substitutes. I gather the Gaffer said something on the lines of "I'm glad you're fit; we're going to need all the support we can get."

Whilst those two experienced players were devastated – and that was the key to Archie leaving Forest the following season – I was thrilled. Being named on the bench was unbelievable. I went back into the room with skipper John McGovern that lunchtime in great spirits. True to form, despite the excitement of being part of the biggest game in club football in a few hours, I slept like a log.

I got up for our pre-match tea and toast about three hours before kick off and was getting ready for the game when the Gaffer said he wanted a word. "Son, I'm taking you off the bench," he said. "I'm putting John O'Hare on it because it's his last chance to win a trophy." He knew I would be disappointed but said I had plenty of years ahead of me.

I told the Gaffer I was disappointed and asked: "Will I get a medal?" Brian Clough assured me I would and said: "Let's hope it's a winners' one!" Nothing against John O'Hare. He was a great professional who did a very good job for Forest and it honestly wasn't about losing out on a place to him. But age shouldn't have come into the selection. It didn't matter whether I was 17 or 37, I had been told face to face I was included only to have it snatched away.

Nevertheless, I watched with excitement as, despite not being at our fluent best, we beat Malmo 1-0 through a Trevor Francis header on the stroke of half time. The atmosphere was euphoric in the dressing room before Brian Clough gave an unexpected order: "Put all your medals in the middle of the room!"

There was no explanation. Most did as they were told, whilst a few weren't going to let go of their medals after doing so much to win them.

My thought staring at those medals was that none of them belonged to me. I wanted my medal that glorious night in Munich and more than 42 years later I am still waiting!

After winning the European Cup in 1979, I went back to Northampton to Mum and Dad's house for five or six weeks. It was lovely to go back home and be in the village with family and friends. That was the perfect way to switch off before reporting for pre-season training.

In the summer I was part of the England under 18s squad playing in a tournament in Las Palmas which also included Russia. The Gaffer and Pete were given the task of managing the team just for that tournament. The players and the rest of the staff flew out to Spain after being told the Gaffer and Pete were coming out on a later flight. The lads were curious to know what the famous Brian Clough and Peter Taylor were like. "You will soon find out!" I said.

The coach took us training and there was still no sign of them by the end of day one. The other staff were getting worried the following day, asking me when they were coming. I honestly had no idea.

Finally, we were told they would be with us within the next two hours, and all gathered in the meeting room. The Gaffer and Pete walked through the door. The Gaffer nodded at the lads and said: "Gentlemen, good afternoon, lovely to see you" before catching my eye. "Hello, son, it's lovely to see you – how are they looking after you? Come and give me a kiss!" I hesitated and he said "Come on, son, give me a kiss. You normally do!" I did the equivalent of a 'walk of shame' over to the Gaffer to give him a peck on the cheek. Imagine how this made me feel in front of the rest of the lads.

Then, the Gaffer looked around the room and said: "Pete, have you seen him over there? You, son, must be a centre half."

"Yes, Mr Clough," he replied.

"I know you are," the Gaffer went on. "You're that ugly you can't be anything other than a centre half."

After training, we were on the bus with the Gaffer and Pete sitting at the front next to a young lady organising the trip. She lit up a cigarette and the Gaffer said: "Put that bloody fag out!" She apologised, but he told her again and said: "Driver, pull over please, get off my bus now!" So we left the organiser in the middle of nowhere with the rest of the staff gobsmacked.

The other lads said they never expected anything like this with Clive Allen chipping in "Your gaffer's crackers!" I was in a better position to understand his behaviour because I had known him for a few years and knew his ways worked. But, for the others, it was an eye-opening experience. Next day we went out, won a couple of football matches, and won the tournament.

When I say I knew him, I never had any idea which Brian Clough I was going to meet. He could be the nicest of men, but also arrogant and ignorant. He could greet me with 'good morning, son', 'get out of my way, son' or just a blank face.

Everything was going so well for me. At 17 years of age, I was involved with a 'champion' team, playing in Europe and for the England youth team. It was an incredible time for me, the best apprenticeship I could have had.

Pre-season, as usual, involved fitness-work at Wollaton Park. We met at the university, got changed, and went over the road into the park where we ran up hills before going back to the unit for salad and a bowl of soup at lunchtime. Then it was more basic running during the afternoon. Now when I occasionally go to Wollaton Park it brings back good memories of those times.

The Gaffer always struck a balance between physical fitness and giving us some freedom. He didn't mind too much what we did if our minds and bodies were right when it really mattered. The way he handled John Robertson was masterful. He and Pete had plenty of digs at his lifestyle when he wasn't fulfilling his potential but gave him plenty of rope in his prime.

We sat in groups of four on the team coach with Robbo often on my left. As the young player, I looked out for the Gaffer when Robbo had a fag. I elbowed Robbo, he threw the cigarette on the floor, put it out, and tried to waft away the smell before the Gaffer got too close. Brian Clough knew full well his star player liked a fag, but that wasn't an issue if he did his job right on a Saturday. Every player knew his job and was expected to go out and perform – whether he had a pre-match pint or went for a 10-mile run beside the Trent was irrelevant.

Our pre-match meal of steak and toast doesn't stack up with today's advice of taking on board more carbohydrates. But did it affect the way we played? Would today's sports scientists and nutritionists have made John Robertson a better player? That's quite a thought because he was a superstar as he was. As for me, I was naturally a fitness fanatic anyway, but never really thought about nutrition or anything like that.

Although he never over-coached, the Gaffer got his point across almost without us noticing. I soon got the message that, as well as the attacking side of my game, I had to make that 50-yard sprint to track back, tuck in and sometimes stand still. In short, I knew my job.

You had to be a particular type of person and player to play for the Gaffer and Pete. Everybody was treated the same and some struggled with it. To fit in at Forest, you had to buy into the Gaffer's way of doing things. He told his midfielders to get the ball and pass it to Robbo.

Gaffer's signing of Stan Bowles from QPR never quite worked. Stan had endless talent, but manager and player got off to a shaky start and never recovered. I was in the dressing room when the Gaffer came in as usual bouncing the ball and told his new player: "Stanley, when you get the ball give it to Robbo, he can play!" Stan was the only player who gave the Gaffer an answer back.

"What?" he replied. "You mean give the ball to Bowlesy, *he* can play."

Stan had his own way of preparing for games. Unlike today, the players went out individually or in small groups to warm up, but he had other things on his mind. He told an apprentice to go to Ladbrokes at Trent Bridge, put a bet on, and would sit watching the 2pm race on TV before coming out to warm up.

I got on well with Asa Hartford, who was transferred back to Manchester City after only three games, one of several midfielders moved on quickly. Gary Megson seemed to be a nervous wreck whilst he was with us. Just before a friendly against Dundee United, we heard someone being violently sick. When Gary walked through the door eyes bulging, the Gaffer wasn't impressed.

Having played at Blackburn in a League Cup tie, my first league chance came at Bristol City where I scored the equaliser in a 1-1 draw and played well. I was also happy with my display in a 3-1 League Cup win at Middlesbrough, and when we opened our defence of the European Cup with a game against another Swedish side Osters Vaxjo.

I was on the bench for the 2-0 City Ground win but in the side on merit for the second leg. I was very excited about starting my first ever European Cup tie, but there was something in the air that night. It's a strange thing. Sometimes you warm up feeling great, other times you get the feeling it's going to be tough – this was the latter.

I thought I did quite well, having two or three efforts at goal, but we were a goal down in the second half and struggling before I put in a good right wing cross for Tony Woodcock to head the equaliser. That away goal gave us valuable breathing space to ease into the second round.

Having a bite to eat afterwards, the Gaffer said I was 'the best player on the park tonight' and that 'you did superbly well'. That didn't get me into his team for the next game, but altogether I was well pleased with my involvement in that amazing season as I started 19 games and came on as substitute in a further 11.

One such start was in the second leg of our next tie in Europe against Arges Pitesti. That was one of the worst places I've ever been to, but the main reason I was glad to get out of Romania was to keep my distance from Kenny Burns. He blamed me for giving him a bad pass in the second half which resulted in him getting booked. After we won the match to go through to the quarter finals, he followed me into the shower, grabbed me by the throat, and threw me to the floor, saying I 'needed to watch myself'. My 'crime' was costing him money and getting him suspended. For a few weeks afterwards, I ensured I was always on the same side as Kenny in training. Today Kenny and I get on great. It was one of those things that happen in football.

One of the special occasions that season was walking out at Anfield for the second leg of the League Cup semi final. We squeezed home 1—0 at the City Ground and again Liverpool fancied their chances of turning us over. It's difficult to describe how it felt emerging from the tunnel at eye level to see the pitch with 50,000 or so fans packed into the famous stadium. There I was playing against Kenny Dalglish and co in a very important game with Wembley at stake. Again I wasn't fazed. I had a couple of half chances after Robbo's penalty doubled our lead and played my part in the team as we drew 1-1 and qualified for the final for a third successive year.

Charlie George walking through the door in January was another highlight. It took me by surprise when he came on a month's loan. He had been my hero ever since that goal in the cup final against Liverpool. When I saw him, my mouth was so wide open, I could have swallowed him. I couldn't wait to tell him my story of watching that Wembley final as a nine-year-old and idolising him and Arsenal for years afterwards. Now I could be playing in the same team as my hero – yet another surreal moment. Unfortunately, I didn't get the chance to play with Charlie when he got the winner in the first leg of the European Super Cup against Barcelona, but I'm proud to say I had a few minutes up front with him in a league game during his brief stay with us.

I had a very scary time when the Gaffer flew us out to Egypt to play a friendly shortly after we'd been hammered 4-1 at Derby. My first sight of Cairo set the scene, with slums, people sleeping at the side of the streets, and cars driving erratically. Seeing the pyramids was a highlight, but I began to feel very ill back in the hotel room with Bryn Gunn.

Soon I was going from bad to worse, feeling hot and sick and likely to pass out. I told Bryn I needed the club doctor who turned out to be having a drink at the bar with the Gaffer. When Gunny explained my problem, the Gaffer said the doc would come after he had finished his drink. That was no good - I needed to see someone fast. Then the doc came and injected me up the backside. I played in the friendly despite still not feeling great, but came back home with one definite conclusion – no more Cairo for me.

Walking in Amsterdam's famous red-light district before the European Cup semi final against Ajax, Pete put me on the spot. I think he chose me because I was the youngest. There were about 25 of us on the trip and Pete said I should ask at one of the brothels if they would get us all a good deal! So that's what I did. They gave me a quote in gilders which didn't mean much to me. Pete rolled his tongue in his cheek, as he often did, and said we would give that one a miss.

This was yet more of their psychology. There was never any intention of going there, he was relaxing us and taking our mind off the game. It made no difference to the Gaffer whether it was a European Cup final or a friendly, the Gaffer and Pete approached all games the same way.

Our build up to the Hamburg final was upset by an injury to Trevor Francis. That was a major setback. Trevor was an international footballer and on fire at the time. Yet our star striker getting injured against Crystal Palace less than four weeks before the final opened a door for me.

We had a very small squad and very few forwards. All I could do was take my chance when it came. Other candidates to play up front in the final were Stan Bowles, who usually played in midfield, and John O'Hare, 12 months on from his 'last chance of winning a medal'!

The Palace game on May 3 begun a manic run of games that would never happen these days. Our trip to Highbury to face Arsenal two days later was another massive occasion – the first time I played at the famous ground against the team I idolised as a schoolboy. That game finished 0-0, but I knew I played well, forcing great goalkeeper Pat Jennings into a couple of saves.

Next day I wasn't involved as we played a County Cup tie against Notts, on the Friday night I started again when we beat Everton at the City Ground with a last-minute goal by Viv Anderson.

Instead of putting our feet up that weekend, we flew straight out to France to tackle French side Stade Brestois next day in a friendly. I kept the starting shirt as we again won 1-0. Two nights later we wound up our league programme with a 3-1 defeat at Wolves. That meant we played on May 3, 5, 6, 9, 10 and 12, six games in ten days!

There was still one more playing date before the final and that was Robbo's testimonial against Leicester City at the City Ground the following Friday night. I started and Stan was upset to be left out because he was friends with Robbo. I thought then I might just get the shirt for the final because I was playing well, but there was still no guarantee.

The way the Gaffer and Pete handled the next 12 days before the Madrid final was pure genius, but still baffles people when they hear about it.

We were told before the testimonial to again have our passports ready because we were flying out the next day to Majorca, where we stayed from Saturday to Saturday. The lads welcomed the sun, but expected hard physical work to get ready for a massive cup tie. Wrong! The Gaffer showed us his hotel, explained the players were staying at a different one, and left us to it with 'behave yourselves and see you next Saturday!' No curfews or drinking bans, just don't get into any trouble.

We half expected the Gaffer to call us together at some point during the week and he did – for a game of uppers and overs on the beach and last man into the sea! There was no training, no talk about Hamburg. Instead we had fun – a few beers, then a few more, same thing day after day. A good time together and lots of laughs - the kind of trip you expect after the end of the season, not before our most important game.

The European Cup final was barely spoken about. The Germans, a very good side including England's own Kevin Keegan and outstanding full back Manny Kaltz, were strong favourites with the bookies. Yet we treated them the same way we did all our opponents – ignored them.

The talk when we met up with the Gaffer and Pete for the return flight was the England versus Scotland international. Robbo and the boss laid wagers on the result. There was still one more important engagement before the final – Robbo's testimonial dinner at the Commodore. That was on the Sunday night just three days before the final and we were all encouraged to attend and have a good time.

The only condition was we needed to make our own way to East Midlands Airport the following morning for the flight to Madrid. But where was Stan? A few explanations have been offered since, but I don't know the truth. Yes, he was scared of flying, but he went on other trips. So now we were down to 15 players with four subs, including reserve goalkeeper Jim Montgomery. Naturally it crossed my mind that, minus Stan Bowles, I had an even better chance of starting.

We arrived at our Madrid hotel and had a few beers together on the Monday. Still no training! Then on the Tuesday the Gaffer took us for a walk. Peter Shilton got twitchy about his lack of preparation and Jimmy Gordon and I were ordered to volley a few balls at him on a busy roundabout with cars beeping their horns all around us! You couldn't make this up.

Still no talk of Hamburg and Keegan and co. The Gaffer wanted to relax our minds and bodies and not worry about the implications of the final. We got together on match day morning and played seven-a-side – with 15 players we couldn't manage the usual eight versus eight!

Clough and Taylor managed the European Cup final like any other match. Before we left the hotel, Pete took the mickey out of Gaz for his shoes and relaxed us with his comedy routine before they said: 'come on, let's go out and win a game of football'. The older players knew more about the European Cup and its history, but young 'uns like me tend to take most things in their stride. I knew I would be the youngest player to play in a European Cup final, but I was there to do my job – no more, no less.

Gaffer named the side, and I was thrilled to be starting up front with Gaz. No talk at all of changing the tactics despite the loss of Trevor Francis. In media interviews, I spoke about the incredible feeling of being involved in the final with Mum and my sister Angela there. Collecting their tickets, they were more nervous about the game than I was. Then seeing them look so proud afterwards was a lovely moment. Dad came home from a cricket tour the day before the final so stayed in Harpole with the rest of the family to watch the game on ITV.

The sole mention of Keegan was an order not to talk to him. Gaffer told us to ignore him in the tunnel even though he was English. Anyone talking to Kevin Keegan would be fined, he said.

The game started with us playing our usual 4-4-2. Hamburg were getting a lot of the ball and making life difficult for us. After 10 minutes or so, the Gaffer told me to drop back into midfield. I asked the other lads 'where?' and ended up on the right inside Martin O'Neill.

Never in my Forest career did we start with a 4-5-1. The pundits described it as a stroke of genius, presuming this was something we worked on in training, but that wasn't so. It was a tactic the Gaffer and Pete came up with on the spur of the moment and I was left to make it work. Whenever we got the ball up to Gaz, it was my job to get as close as possible to support him.

I was more advanced, when the goal came in the 20th minute to give us such a massive lift. Robbo got possession in his usual position on the left flank and fed it into Gaz who ended up in a heap on the floor yet, managed to hook it back to Robbo in a more central position. The maestro stroked the ball towards the far post and it ended up in the back of the net. Euphoria! We huddled together to celebrate. You can just about see my number ten shirt with arms all around me. Hamburg then had a goal disallowed almost straightaway. These days it might have been given. Back then, a lad was standing offside before the ball was slotted past Shilts, so the goal was chalked off.

What a performance we put on that night! Not everyone appreciated the way we played. We had very little of the ball, but it was an outstanding effort out of possession. Gaz ran three marathons up front on his own to keep Hamburg's defenders occupied, whilst I was mostly in the midfield five and the back four did their stuff. Shilts was unbeatable, pulling off several wonderful saves.

I worked and worked. I tell my players now you can have a great game without touching the ball and I highlight the Hamburg game. Everyone in English football knew how difficult it was to get back at us once we were in front and we played that to perfection in Madrid. We had no choice but to stop Hamburg playing and that's what we did.

Most of my work was defensive but, in the second half, I went on a long lung-bursting run to just outside the Hamburg box where I let fly. Unfortunately, it was with my left foot and it flew into the stands. The Gaffer pulled me off in the 68th minute. I didn't want to come off, but I could see his thinking. "Come and sit next to me," he said as he relied on the experience of John O'Hare to try to see out the game.

The lads continued where I left off, keeping Hamburg at bay despite waves and waves of attacks. We fought for our lives. A goal for Hamburg at any stage could easily have ruined all the hard slog we put in. I was sat with remaining subs Dave Needham, Bryn Gunn, and Jim Montgomery, when left back Frank Gray collapsed in a heap with a few minutes of normal time left.

As Gunny warmed up, his motivation from Clough and Taylor was, "We're in the shit now!" You couldn't make it up! But, as always, Gunny went on and was superb as we stayed firm until the final whistle. We were European champions again!

Never underestimate the massive heart, discipline, and backs-to-the-wall effort we all put into winning that trophy. I rate that as one of our best performances during those glory years. We were magnificent.

We had great players and were a great team. I still get sick of people saying Forest would not win it now. There are many huge clubs in England who have never won Europe's premier club trophy and we did it twice! There I was still only 18 years of age with two European Cup wins under my belt.

The feeling afterwards was incredible. Feelings that will never go away. I can honestly say winning those trophies mean more to me every year that goes by. Being involved not only with great footballers, but great blokes, was more than I could have dreamt of. And all this before my career had even started.

The Gaffer caused yet another surprise by insisting that, as we won the cup together, we would celebrate together as a team. That meant no going out on the town, but a quiet night at the hotel. My way of marking conquering Europe was a game of Connect 4, a bite to eat, and a few drinks. Some of the lads weren't having it. They waited for the Gaffer and Pete to go to their rooms and disappeared into the night. I wasn't one of them.

I further celebrated the European Cup win by going on a camping holiday with my brothers, sister, and a couple of mates. One night we were outside having a couple of drinks when someone came up to me and punched me in the face. I must have done the 100m again in 11 seconds. My brother Martyn sorted him out before the police arrived, so we ended up down at the station where one of the officers said: "Aren't you, Gary Mills who just played in the European Cup final?"

CHAPTER 4
THREE YEARS THAT CHANGED MY WORLD

By ALAN HUDSON, *former player and assistant coach of Seattle Sounders*

I had lost touch with English football when manager Alan Hinton took me back to look at some players. We watched a reserve game at Nottingham Forest and ended up signing Peter Ward and Gary Mills.

Ward lit up the American game and Gary did a really good job for us. He was a winger but there was more to his game as he could cut inside and had serious pace. Gary had some niggly injuries, probably not helped by the astroturf.

At 20, Gary was younger than the other English players at Seattle and playing on the other side of the world took guts. He was level headed, a bit naïve and I thought he would make it even bigger than he did such as playing for England – although there can be several reasons for that.

Gary was part of a major achievement in Seattle's history when we reached the Soccer Bowl final. I have lots of discussions about the NASL but the standard back then was very high.

The New York Cosmos team, with all their international superstars, we played in the final would have held their own in the top three in the old First Division. There was nothing in that game which we lost 1-0 on a bad pitch in San Diego.

The club then got new owners, sacked Alan Hinton and, when I was relieved of the captaincy, I realised my time was up. I understand what Gary says about the new manager because things were going downhill.

*****

DURING those early years at Forest, I liked the Gaffer. There was no reason not to. He taught me a lot about the game and introduced me to a hugely successful team. He was also great to my family, making them feel part of my fast-developing career.

The next phase of my time with the Gaffer was more mixed and left me with a question I don't think will ever be answered: Did I have one spell at Forest or two? I don't know to this day why I went on loan to Derby and why the Gaffer treated me so coldly after I returned from Seattle Sounders with a broken leg.

The 1980/81 season was always going to be massive for me. After being in and around the team for almost two years, could I now kick on and become a regular?

My bonus from winning the European Cup helped fund a Ford Capri, my first car after successfully passing my driving test. Nan and Pap's council house in Harpole was available at a discounted price of £2,000 and they urged me to buy that for less than I spent on the car.

I still think today 'what a fool' when I drive past that house. Typically, the Gaffer ensured I kept my feet on the ground by insisting he didn't want to see my car in the Forest car park. He told me to keep travelling by bus or get a lift with one of the lads. Whenever I drove into the City Ground, I kept my car hidden from view.

It was always going to be a big ask to follow up the success of the previous two seasons, particularly knowing Trevor Francis was out until around Christmas. Our pre-season tour of America, Canada, and Columbia was a mixed bag. Rather than helping to get us match fit, the lifestyle contributed to several players putting on weight. I had never been to America before, but food was on tap, including steak and eggs for breakfast, and portions the likes of which I had never seen before. In addition, 24-hour room service was available.

A trip of eating and drinking, sandwiched between playing games, resulted in all of us putting on a few pounds and big Larry Lloyd putting on a few more. Jimmy Gordon called Lloydy a 'disgrace' to which he responded: "It's not that bad, Jimmy, I could soon shift them after a good shit."

It was roasting hot in Tampa Bay, but an even hotter reception in Columbia, another place I will never go back to. We were greeted with stones, bricks and boulders as we emerged from the tunnel for a friendly. It was no better on the pitch as home players seemed intent on injuring us. It was horrible and, to make it worse, we were 5-0 down by half time.

The lads agreed they didn't want to go back out for the second half.

We wanted out of there as quickly as possible with no more damage. Pete insisted we complete the game by continually passing the ball back to Shilts to see out the 90 minutes. That's what we did as the crowd booed and abused us. The game ended 5-0. Columbia was a rude culture shock, especially after being treated so well in Tampa and Vancouver.

Even getting out of Columbia was a hassle. Our bags were already on the plane when we were told our next friendly was off. That went down very well with the lads as none of us were looking forward to going to Ecuador. So we scrambled around to get our luggage, with the news we were bound for Miami instead being very popular.

We also travelled in pre-season to Bayern Munich and Zurich, for a game arranged as part of the Raimondo Ponte transfer, before opening up the league season with a 2-0 defeat at Spurs. Ponte was Forest's first foreign signing from Grasshoppers Zurich after playing against us in the European Cup. That provided me with more competition for a midfield place. Raimondo liked to kiss players if either we or he scored which was a bit of a culture shock. We were more used to a hug or a slap on the back.

I was on the bench a few times before starting for the first time in a league cup tie at Peterborough, where I partnered Gaz up front in a 3-0 victory. Soon afterwards I scored a couple of goals at Bury where Raimondo got a hat trick and we won 7-0. Overall, it proved a tough season with some setbacks along the way. After playing at Wembley for the previous three seasons, including two League Cup wins, it was a shock playing in a side hammered 4-1 at Watford.

Worse was to come in the European Cup. The lads thrived on battling facilities, travelling, and our opponents, and were looking forward to another season of European challenges. But that all went out of the window when we lost 1-0 away and at home to Bulgarian side CSKA Sofia in the first round. We were all shocked and disappointed but there was no bollocking from the Gaffer. It was all about getting on with the next challenge.

More setbacks followed, losing the European Super Cup on away goals to Valencia, and travelling to Tokyo in midweek where we lost the world championship to Uruguayan side Nacional. The Gaffer left me and Gunny behind as we had an important FA Cup match less than three days later at the City Ground. I started and we scored late on to beat Bristol City 2-1.

It was in January 1981 when I first met my future wife Sue. Some of us had been for a few drinks on Sunday lunchtime at The White Hart at Arnold. The group included Viv Anderson, Pedro Richards from Notts County, Walshy, and Gaz Birtles. Then, for some reason, Viv suggested we go out at night as well. I wasn't that keen because we hardly ever went out on a Sunday night, but got talked into it as we met up at The Dog and Bear in town, before going on to the Uriah Heap. It was there that I set eyes on a very good-looking girl. I chatted to Forest fan Clive Whiting, a friend of hers, and asked who she was. He said her name was Sue and invited her over. That wasn't what I expected, but Clive introduced us, and the rest, as they say, is history. I asked her out during the week, and she agreed. Imagine my disappointment when she didn't turn up. I thought she must have changed her mind. But then I got a message that she had been unable to make it and we made another arrangement. Sue Staniforth, as she was known then, didn't know anything about me as a footballer. I think it was my legs that attracted her, or so she tells me! As for me, she was a very good-looking girl.

Back on the field, our last remaining hope of silverware was in the FA Cup and we were pleased to be drawn at home in the quarter final, albeit against a very good Ipswich Town side. That was a hell of a game, with us coming back from two goals down to lead 3-2. I was switched to right back when Viv dislocated his shoulder just before half time, and I was involved in Ipswich's equaliser as a shot took a deflection off me and looped over Shilts.

But the Gaffer was impressed enough with what he saw to say afterwards: "I think you're going to be a full back, son." History was repeating itself from my time with England Schoolboys. I never thought of myself as a defender but, from then on, I spent most of my career at full back or wing back.

Don McLeod had left the club and Walshy moved in with Darron Gee, who when I went into management became my regular assistant. I went to live in digs in Silverdale for a few weeks before moving to the Forest Hills Hotel. Dave and Carol Langford had bought it from Alan Hill and asked me whether I'd like to live there. I did for six months, and during this time Dave, Carol, and her Dad George really looked after me, before a room became available at Sue's house.

Whilst living in the hotel I had a bright idea – I wanted a perm. Sue's mum Val was a hairdresser and agreed to do it for me. I looked in the mirror and quite liked it – not bad at all! But when I got back to the hotel that night, I noticed my hair had expanded a few inches. I knew I was in for a ribbing at training, so I tried to cover it up as best I could. I filled the sink with water and wet my hair so it looked ok. It's amazing how quickly your hair dries though, and walking down Musters Road I could feel it getting drier so I popped into a shop and poured a bottle of water over my head.

That did the trick for a while, but back in the dressing room the lads started laughing at me. It was getting drier and worse all the time. The Gaffer and Pete were talking about the game when the Gaffer said: "Never mind the game, what about his f---ing hair? It's a disgrace. What have you f---ing done, son?" I said I was sorry, but he went on: "Oh my f---ing God, look at the state of him!"

Fortunately, my face (if not my hair) fitted for most of that season. I featured in 40 games and bagged 11 goals as Forest finished seventh in the First Division – disappointing only because of what had gone before. The Gaffer confirmed I was very much in his plans as we talked at the end of the season about a new contract. I said I'd love to sign, and he showed me a largely blank piece of paper with the order: 'sign here'. He said it was a three-year deal and refused to answer my questions about money. "Leave it to me, just sign it. You trust me, don't you?" he added. I agreed to sign the blank contract but, before I did, asked about the European Cup final medal I was still waiting for. "I told you I would get you that medal," he said.

"Ok, great," I answered, again putting my trust in him. The medal was as important, in my eyes, as signing that contract.

That was the end of the negotiations. I was on £100 a week when I signed professional forms on my 17th birthday, with a £20 a week increase each season. When I picked up the envelope my new deal was the same. Money wasn't the issue. I had established myself in the England youth set up and was playing more and more often for Forest. Being offered a three-year contract meant the world to me.

Talking of England, a few days with the under 21s, being managed by Terry Venables, and a game against Norway led to an interesting session with the Gaffer. Back at Forest for training, he asked how it had gone.

"The coaching was really good, Gaffer," I replied.

"Coaching? F---ing coaching? I will show you f---ing coaching."

He asked me to get him a ball, then we walked down the tunnel and onto the City Ground pitch. He held the ball above his head and threw it to my feet. "That's how to take a throw in - now that's f---ing coaching." Next he kicked the ball to me. "That's how to pass a ball – that's f---ing coaching." Next on the list was heading and he continued showing me the basics until saying: "Don't you ever talk to me about f---ing coaching."

My comments, never intended as criticism of Forest's coaching methods, stuck with him for weeks.

The way we played at Forest was to pass and be comfortable with the ball in an attacking sense. We were told to turn when we could to put the opposition on the back foot. Our 'coaching' was little more than 'defenders are paid to head and kick the ball out of our penalty area, and forwards to put the ball in the opposition's net.' It honestly was as simple as that.

My job, as a right sided midfield player or winger, was to put the ball into the opposition's box. Later as a full back, I had to 'stop the cross'. The Gaffer shouted that message constantly at both full backs. He knew that if teams kept putting the ball into the box, forwards made their runs to the near post, and midfielders got themselves into the penalty area, they would score goals.

As we looked to get back to trophy-winning ways at the start of the 1981-82 campaign, there was a new face at the City Ground in £1m striker Justin Fashanu. Unfortunately, things never really got going for Justin at Forest. I was there that day when the Gaffer threw him off the training ground when he turned up with his agent for another unforgettable conversation.

Former club Norwich were showing an interest in taking him back and I was in the Gaffer's office when Justin knocked at the door.

After the not unusual welcome of 'what the f--- do you want?', Justin, who had recently told the world he was a born-again Christian, said: "I've been talking to God and he told me I shouldn't go back to Norwich."

Quick as a flash, the Gaffer answered: "There's only one God in Nottingham and I'm saying that you are!" Colin Walsh and I were in stitches, with no disrespect to Fash.

Justin was a lad I got on well with, having already met as part of the England Under 21 side. It's true his Goal of the Season for Norwich against Liverpool didn't do him any harm, but he had earned his big money transferring to a club like Forest for being the First Division's top scorer. I can't put my finger on why it never happened for him, but I guess, if Justin was still with us now, he'd admit he could have done better. In the end he only stayed at Forest for a season and his next stop was Southampton on loan, rather than Norwich, before he added a long and varied list of clubs to his CV.

The guy intrigued me with his toiletry bag full of oils and hair and beauty products, his BMW, and having an agent – I swear I didn't know what an agent was when he told me. I also didn't know much about Justin's upbringing back then. For whatever reason, neither he nor Peter Ward, whom I became particularly good friends with, made it at Forest where demands and expectations were still sky high after our recent success.

The Gaffer surprised me during that season by telling me to go home and spend a couple of weeks with my Mum and Dad. I didn't know why and am still guessing now. Perhaps he thought I was becoming too big for my boots and needed grounding. I'm not that kind of person, but it's almost impossible to have experienced what I had at an early age and be unaffected. My parents and Nan and Pap were curious, thinking I must have done something wrong. The Gaffer never said anything even after I returned to the City Ground.

Forest were midtable and the season was meandering towards the end when the Gaffer pulled me and Wardy into his office and surprised us. "How would you like to go to America, son?" he asked. "America?" I'd never thought about it. This was when there was much razzamatazz about the American game with dancing girls, barbecues in the car park, and plenty of foreigners, including well-known English players.

The idea was to join Seattle Sounders for pre-season in March and spend six months out there. This needed thinking about for several reasons, not least my flourishing relationship with Sue. I was still living in her family home and the prospect of leaving her for six months wasn't what I had in mind. Wardy had already said yes and strongly urged me to go to Seattle with him. Going together would be much better, he said. Football-wise the move was a big shock – I was in and around the Forest team that season, playing 17 league and cup games and being involved right up to the time I got on the plane.

Seattle were managed by Alan Hinton, the former Forest and Derby winger, who knew the Gaffer very well from his playing days. The deal, as I understood it, was that I was going there on loan as I was still under contract at Forest. I was a bit worried that the American season lasted until September as I'd miss the first six weeks of the new campaign at Forest, but the Gaffer made light of it. "It will do you good, son," he said.

Wardy thought the move was good for him. He was 26 years old and hadn't settled too well at Forest after being a legend at Brighton. For me, aged 20, it was an even bigger step to move to America on my own and live in another country. The deal though was unbelievable. I was loaned a five-litre sports car almost as big as a house and use of an apartment with a swimming pool and sauna. There were big financial plusses going to America although the money side of it was never the issue. The pound was worth $1.95 which made a lot of difference to my weekly wage. I also got a healthy signing on fee which helped me get my own place and set myself up financially back in England.

Sue never stopped crying and it wasn't easy for me either. But the decision was made. Wardy and I stayed in a hotel in London before flying from Heathrow the following day, but in the morning Alan Hinton told me I'd been selected again for England Under 21s, so did I want to stay in England and join up with Seattle a few days later? I wanted to be involved with England but didn't want to confuse things any further.

Although there were perks of going to the States, it was no holiday. We worked very hard out there to compete in a high standard of football.

After I'd been in America for a few weeks, Alan Hinton , my new gaffer, softened the blow by asking if Sue would like to come out for three or four weeks in June.

Meanwhile I was getting used to Seattle's amazing Kingdome 100,000 indoor seater stadium and there were plenty of English faces around besides Wardy. Roger Davies, the former Derby striker, Steve Daley, who commanded a world record transfer fee when moving from Wolves to Manchester City, former Crystal Palace player Paul Hammond, Ray Evans from Stoke, and Bolton Wanderers stalwart Roy Greaves were all part of the set up.

The big name as far as I was concerned however was Alan Hudson. Playing alongside him was another surreal moment. A few years earlier Huddy and Charlie George had been my heroes. I'd already played briefly in the same team as Charlie, now I was Huddy's teammate.

The apartment was beautiful, and when they brought me my sports car, I was no longer asking whether I'd done the right thing. Pre-season included going to the training ground in the morning – a place next to where Boeing made planes but fortunately, we could hardly hear a thing – followed by an afternoon swim in the pool.

I was given the number 11 shirt with my name on the back – another novelty – and my introduction to the fans was slightly different from at Forest. We all ran onto the pitch individually to announcements more like a boxing match. "He's quick, he's like lightning, he's the wizard on the wing - Gary Mills!" Imagine how good that made me feel.

We sung the American national anthem before every game and the football itself was of excellent standard. Things were soon going well for Wardy and me on and off the field. The team picked up results and we found a couple of bars to relax in, along with the drive-throughs where we put money in a slot in the wall for a hamburger.

Alan Hinton was a good man manager who inherited some of the best aspects of the Gaffer. He helped make the dressing room a happy place. We played and socialised together and got the balance right. As at Forest, when we trained we worked very hard, but Alan Hinton kept the game simple and didn't over coach. In my opinion, not boring the players shitless on the training pitch was a positive.

Wolverhampton's Kenny Hibbitt joined us, along with Nicky Reid, from Manchester City. We also had an American lad, Mark Peterson, playing up front with Wardy and both scored goals for fun. After the home games, we'd 'go on the road'. That usually meant nine or ten days away taking in a couple of games with a lot of travelling. We flew to the likes of New York Cosmos on the other side of America, and then to Portland in Canada for another game.

Sue enjoyed her month out in the States after a strange incident when I met her at the airport. She had lost so much weight I barely recognised her getting off the plane and my first call was to take her to an 'all you can eat' Pizza restaurant to fatten her up. When our time together in paradise came to an end, it consoled her that it would only be a couple of months before I flew back for good. But fate took a hand.

We qualified for the end-of-season play offs against Fort Lauderdale in a two-legged tie. We were trailing by one goal going into the last minute of the second leg when Wardy did well on the left side, Roger Davies produced a brilliant header back across goal at the far post, and Kenny Hibbitt plunged in to net a diving header. I had been 10 seconds away from planning my journey home, instead we had a third game with Fort Lauderdale to play, which also reached a dramatic conclusion. The game was scoreless after 90 minutes and went into sudden death overtime when Kenny again became the hero by netting a spectacular volley.

That made my stay even longer, and the club were good to me again by inviting Sue to come out for the Soccer Bowl final. This was quite an undertaking on her part, flying over to San Francisco on her own, then getting on a six-seater plane for the journey to San Diego, but she agreed to come.

There was a very memorable event the night before the game when both teams were invited to a gala pre-match dinner with the great Pele, who had previously played for our opponents in the final, New York Cosmos, as guest of honour. This meant getting kitted out in suits and dicky bow ties, which didn't work out well for Kenny. His trousers were the wrong size, only coming halfway up his legs. He was very worried about the photographs, but the lads told him he could stand in the middle and nobody would notice. That was until we all went our separate ways and left Kenny to face the music!

Kenny made me laugh when he was introduced to Pele, telling him in his Yorkshire accent: "Tell you what, you weren't a bad player!"

I had my photograph taken with Pele, a great honour to go along with the shirt from fellow Brazilian legend Carlos Alberto when Cosmos visited the Kingdome.

Unfortunately, there were no late reprieves for us in the final after Italian striker Giorgio Chinaglio scored the only goal for Cosmos. As well as the former Brazilian captain, famous Dutchman Johan Neeskens was also in the winning team. We were completely gutted to lose after battering New York in the first half without getting ourselves in front.

It had been a magnificent season for me at Seattle, I loved every minute. I got the opportunity to play and fly all over America and Canada. It was a great experience, seeing amazing cities such as New York, Chicago, Montreal, Vancouver, San Diego, and Fort Lauderdale to name just a few.

But one flight to Fort Lauderdale in particular will stay with me forever. Everything was fine until suddenly, without warning, the plane dropped thousands of feet. It was chaos, with stewardesses thrown everywhere and people screaming. I thought my life was coming to an end.

I have never seen so many grown up men crying, and I was one of them. I got hold of Peter Ward's hand and wouldn't let go. Luckily we survived, but for a long time afterwards I found flying very difficult.

We flew back to Seattle after the final and were preparing to travel back to England, when Wardy pulled me to one side and said Alan Hinton had told him there was a problem with me returning to Forest. It had something to do with the number of loan players at Seattle but didn't make much sense to me. Nobody at Forest or Seattle had spoken to me about it.

Dad arranged to meet us back at Heathrow Airport, but when we walked into the arrivals lounge the whole family was there waiting, along with my new niece Gemma, my sister's first child. It was such a lovely surprise, typical of my family.

I turned up at the City Ground ready for a fresh start at Forest, but my reunion with the Gaffer was very strange. When I went into his office he gave me a hug and said: "I've heard how well you have done at Seattle but unfortunately, son, you can't play for me this season." Although Wardy had warned me, it was still a shock. When I asked why, he just said it was 'paperwork not done properly'.

"What do I do now?" I asked. It was September and the season had started.

He said: "Leave it with me, we will find you a club to play for on loan." Two days later, much to my surprise, Alan Hinton was with the Gaffer in his office and the boss said: "What about going back to America, son, next March – and I can get you to Derby County on loan?" Mentioning Derby, Forest's biggest rivals, was a big shock in itself.

Perhaps here I can set the record straight for Forest fans. I had no other intention when I came back to England than playing for Nottingham Forest. The last thing I expected was to be moving along the A52 and playing in the Second Division.

I had been so excited about putting on a red shirt again after signing my three-year deal at Forest. I had just been involved in two European Cups wins and a Soccer Bowl final – three massive occasions in successive years – whilst still a young man of 20. Now I wanted to establish myself in the Forest side as my career was thriving. For that to be taken away from me, through no fault of my own, hurt. I was pushed into a decision I never wanted to make.

I went away for a couple of days to speak to Sue about another massive call. I didn't want to go back to America without her. So my way of proposing was to say 'let's get married' and you can come with me - and she agreed. Then I sat down with Alan Hinton to agree terms, including a bigger signing on fee to compensate for what had happened.

Later in my career I would have stood up for myself and asked more questions, but the Gaffer was difficult to say no to. Derby were the only club offered to me and I got on extremely well with manager John Newman when I spoke with him. John was a particularly nice guy – which isn't a qualification for a football manager – but made it easier to go to the Baseball Ground. The 'loan' aspect also raises questions in my mind now. Many players have moved from Forest to Derby and vice versa over the years, but I don't remember many, if any, loan deals.

Going to Derby was a shock to the system. I'd only known success during my first few years in professional football, now I was playing for a side struggling near the bottom of the Second Division, and a manager trying to keep his job. Although I went to Derby unexpectedly, I gave my all every time I put on a Rams shirt. John Newman singled me out for praise in the dressing room after a game against Grimsby as an example of the effort and commitment we needed.

It was a sad moment for me when he was sacked, but I was thrilled when Peter Taylor walked through the door. I always got on well with Pete, in many ways better than I did with the Gaffer. Pete encouraged me, told me I was a good player, and made me feel special. I think he believed in me more than Brian Clough did.

I probably didn't take in just what it meant at the time. Pete had 'retired' after suffering from a heart attack, and left Forest. Then about six months later he became Derby County manager. We are talking here about the famous rift between the duo that was never resolved right up to Pete's death. I can only write from what I saw and experienced, and the Gaffer and Pete were a team. Pete had never been my boss at Forest but was the one who cracked the jokes and made us feel at ease. He was a much funnier man than I think he knew.

Pete was delighted to see me that day. He had a big smile on his face and said something on the lines of 'well, who would have believed this?' For me, it meant a shift from being more friendly, to knowing he was the gaffer, and I went on to enjoy my few months at the Baseball Ground very much.

November 11 was already a red-letter day – my 21st birthday – but with a wedding to come, we took it a stage further and had an engagement party as well! Mum managed The Red Lion pub just off junction 16 of the M1, so that was the ideal venue. She did us proud with a massive buffet and, as well as celebrating my life-long love with Sue, I also made another great friend. I asked my brother Martyn if he knew anyone to do a disco and he recommended Polly, real name Raymond, whom I'd never met before. He helped make it a party not to forget – and one we never wanted to end. I remember slipping him another £10 note at midnight, saying it was a great night and could he continue for another hour. That happened another two or three times and we finished around 4am! Polly has since become one of my best mates.

The wedding date was set for March 1983 in Ruddington, Nottinghamshire, but in the meantime, there was plenty to do on the pitch. I played 23 league and cup games for Derby, bagging myself a couple of goals. The first was the most memorable – a

Never without a ball: I always looked forward to our family holidays to Swanage and Butlins.

Pictured front with ball, I eventually made the
team at Harpole Primary School.

Here I am third from left on front row with the famous
Harpole Trueshots, the club I helped to form. My brother
Martyn is top right and a young Graham, our mascot, with
the ball next to me.

My Pap Frost pictured left on back row with
Harpole FC in 1933/4.

My Dad Roly is in the middle of the front row with
the ball lining up for Harpole FC.

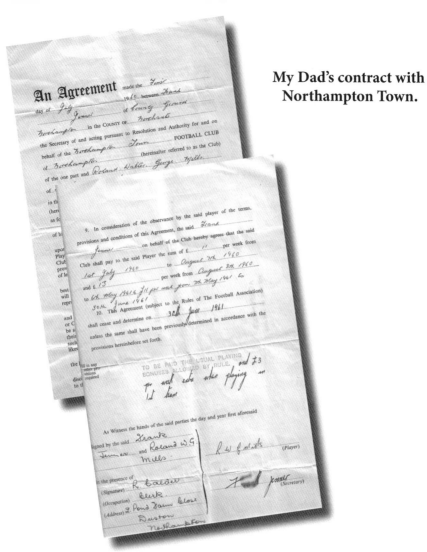

My Dad's contract with Northampton Town.

I was scouted by Nottingham Forest while playing for Long Buckby.

**My first taste of glory: Winning the Umbro
trophy with Long Buckby.**

**Leader of the pack: With my friends from
Bugbrooke Campion school.**

International honours: I'm third from left on the front row before scoring two tries at Twickenham for England Schoolboys in 1978.

The programme from my big day against Portugal at Twickenham.

Dad was very proud
when I was selected for
England Schoolboys at
football in 1977.

**Celebrating my goal for England Schoolboys
against Scotland at Wembley.**

After my achievements in football, rugby and athletics, I chose to sign as an apprentice at Nottingham Forest at the age of 16.

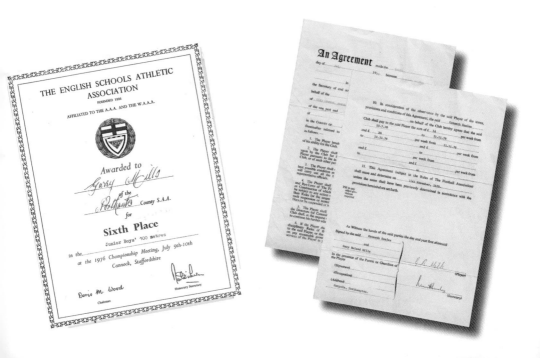

I was 16 when I made my First Division debut against Arsenal in 1978 and three days later I was on the bench against Liverpool in the European Cup (below right).

FOOTBALL LEAGUE DIVISION ONE—SATURDAY 9th September 1978

FOREST v ARSENAL OFFICIAL MATCH-DAY PROGRAMME PRICE 20p

FOREST REVIEW

FOREST

Mills tipped for World Cup

Gary Mills

GARY Mills, the Harpole youngster who will launch into the super income bracket by signing for Nottingham Forest today, could be playing in the 1982 World Cup for England.

So says Forest manager Brian Clough in his national newspaper column today.

Gary, who was 17 last Saturday and was playing for Long Buckby Juniors only a few months ago, and his father Roly met Clough today to discuss the terms of his contract with the all-conquering Forest team, who last lost a league game a year ago tomorrow.

Says Clough: ". . . the failure risk (in football) IS high. One thousand and twenty-one lads might not make it — for it is a hard road to tread. But Gary Mills could be the 1,022nd!

"Last Saturday there was a very mature World Cup player called Ardiles in action against Nottingham Forest. He cost £325,000 . . . Now Idaon't want to prejudice Gary Mills or his dad before they start talking to me but Gary celebrated his birthday that day. And, in his first full league game, he matched Ardiles, and sometimes he outplayed him.

"When I look at Gary Mills I realise that we have a head start on Argentina already for the 1982 World Cup. We have to qualify to go to Spain, while they go as holders. But in all their population have they got an apprentice like him coming through? No, they haven't."

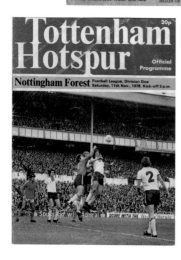

I had a fantastic 17th birthday at White Hart Lane where I outshone World Cup winner Ossie Ardiles.

In action for Forest against Everton.

Champions of Europe in Madrid - what a feeling!

Doing a Nobby Stiles-like dance celebrating our famous victory at the Bernabeu Stadium.

Two European Cups, but just one medal.

I was paid just £120 a week when
I started in the European
Cup final in 1980!

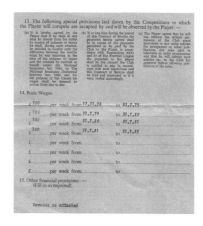

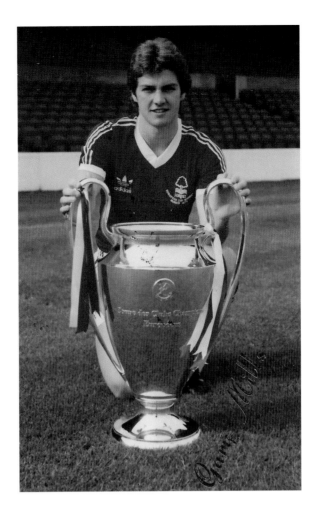

Me with the European Cup at the City Ground.

Gary's family thrilled at European Cup win

Gary's family watch the match. Left to right in front are his grandparents Tom and Kathleen Frost, his father Roly and his brother Graham. Behind is his brother Martyn.

My proud family cheered me on to European glory.

The all-conquering Forest team in 1980.

The lads back together almost 40 years later.

CHRIS TURNER · ALAN HUDSON · IAN BRIDGE · PAUL HAMMOND   TONY CRUDO · CRAIG NICHOLSON · FRANK BARTON
(Assistant Player/Coach)

DON GREHERT · GARY McGUIRE · KENNY HIBBITT · GARY MILLS · ROY GREAVES · BENNY DYROLE · ROBBIE ZIPP · STEVE DALEY · ROGER DAVIES · ALAN HINTON · JEFF STOCK · BRIAN SCHMETZER
(Trainer)   (Equipment Manager)   (Team Manager/Head Coach)

FRED HAMEL · STEVE BUTTLE · NICKY REID   BOBBY HOWE · RAY EVANS
MARK PETERSON · PETER WARD   (Assistant Coach)

I enjoyed a great first season with Seattle.

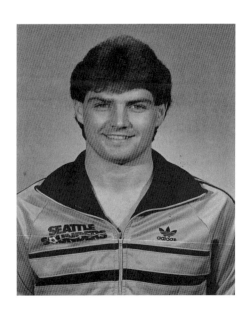

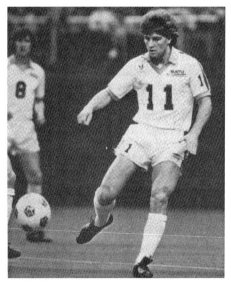

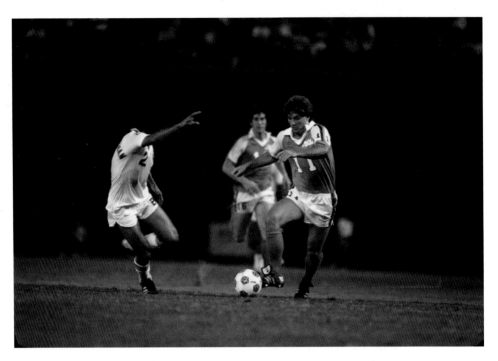

With Seattle Sounders, wearing 11, playing in the Soccer Bowl final against New York Cosmos.

Sounder Gary Mills is examined after breaking his right leg in a collision with Vancouver's Dave Watson, No. 3 at right. Mills will be out for eight weeks.

Former England defender Dave Watson, right, looks away after I suffered my horrific leg break in my second season at Seattle.

On right of back row whilst on loan at Derby County
during which I marked John Robertson out of the
game in a 2-0 FA Cup win over Forest.

Returning to Forest in 1983. I'm standing
on the right of the back row.

Mills-a player of many parts

GARY MILLS, a European Cup finalist with us in Madrid, hasn't had too many disappointments in his short career in the game.

But I dare say he's still wondering why there have been occasions he has been left out of an England youth squad when he was good enough to play in our first team at Nottingham Forest.

I am certain that not being included by England hit him as hard as it could hit anyone — even though the young man has a remarkable even temperament.

There was an occasion, too, when I asked to keep him back from England duty because I needed him. So one way or another he has had to make some sacrifices to make his way with one of the top clubs in the country.

The alternative is to do what Stephen Burke decided . . . and that's seek a transfer. In my opinion, he was badly advised about his future, pressed for a move and ended up being sold to Queen's Park Rangers less than 12 months ago for a fee of about £150,000.

Stephen couldn't see himself making headway at Forest as long as John Robertson's legs could carry him but had he stayed on he might not have got

Below: Gary Mills shrugs off a challenge from Liverpool's Kenny Dalglish.

Forest boss BRIAN CLOUGH writes for you

a chance of playing in a European Cup Final.

That's exactly what happened to Gary Mills, who didn't look at things in the short term but more to a 10 or 15 year future.

It's history now that Gary took over from a £1 million player and did his stuff in a match that had seasoned pros quaking in their sponsored boots!

Not only did he come out of the final with credit, it has got to be remembered the demands that we put on his inexperienced shoulders. The importance of the match has got to be taken into consideration — and so too has the fact that he was up and down from one position to another like a yo-yo.

But wherever he was he made an attempt to fulfil the responsibilities of the role. If we'd sent him to full back I'm absolutely certain he would have made a reasonable show of

things . . . and that's not something that the vast majority of players could do.

Had we asked our England defender Viv Anderson, who is a highly accomplished full back, to go to centre forward he would probably have looked a novice. And that's no indictment against Viv — just an indication of Gary's versatility.

And, before you ask . . . No, I don't think Gary is going to be one of those players of many parts who end up with no fixed position. He's still learning his trade at the moment and I still don't know where he is likely to finish up.

All I do know is that if he continues to make the kind of progress he has done in the last couple of years, there's got to be a place for him somewhere.

If anything it's all too easy for him at the moment. If we stick him out wide on the right he does everything expected of him and has something in reserve. If we put him in midfield he ends up running the show and in attack all he is short of is a goal or two.

But all I'm asking next season is to see further development from him. Of course, much depends whether we sign anyone but no matter who comes in, Gary is here to stay.

Brian Clough

MATCH WEEKLY

I felt ten feet tall when I read this article from the Gaffer.

RANGERS AGREE £150,000 DEAL FOR MILLS

SOUNESS BACK IN BUSINESS!

GRAEME SOUNESS has swooped for yet another English player.

Big-spending Rangers last night agreed to pay £150,000 for Nottingham Forest's mid-field man Gary Mills.

The former England under-21 player will talk to Souness in Nottingham today before making a decision.

by BOB HARRIS

Jigsaw

If the move goes through as expected Mills will join the party of English players already in Glasgow, including Terry Butcher, Graham Roberts, Chris Woods, Colin West and Neil Woods.

Souness has been in England negotiating for new players for most of the week. He already has a £400,000 bid for Oxford's Ray Houghton on the table — ironically, Celtic have also made an attempt to sign the same

player in the last two days.

Souness has been told by Oxford that they will not sell until the end of the season, which prompted the offer yesterday for Mills.

The Scot has been searching for a right-side mid-field man and believes Mills can complete the jigsaw.

The 25-year-old has been in and out of the Forest side since making his debut in 1978. He also played for Seattle Sounders and, briefly, Derby County.

He has suffered sometimes because of his versatility, as he is able to fill in anywhere down his natural right side. This season he has performed just as well on the left flank.

So close to joining Glasgow Rangers but it wasn't to be.

25-yarder into the top corner against QPR who included former Northampton Town player, and later Derby manager, John Gregory, in their side. The game against Leeds, however, sticks in my mind for all the wrong reasons with visiting fans ripping out seats in some of the worst scenes I ever experienced in my career, whilst the happiest memory was in the third round of the FA Cup.

Of all the teams we could draw it had to be Forest at the Baseball Ground. My immediate thoughts were mixed. It was a big occasion, but I thought I wouldn't be allowed to play. Usually there is a clause in a loan contract to say you can't play against your parent club, and I had no reason to believe the Gaffer was going to do Pete any favours!

But Pete told me there was no problem and I was playing. I've thought this over plenty of times since – most notably when writing this book – and I still can't be sure why this happened. Maybe the Gaffer didn't rate me as a danger to Forest that day? The thought crossed my mind. There was no contact from Forest – not a dicky bird – from the moment I walked out of training at the City Ground until after I returned from America, so I can only guess.

We met up as a team at the hotel before the match for something I hadn't experienced much at Forest – a tactical discussion! I'd been playing on the right side of midfield, but Pete took me to one side that lunchtime and said he wanted 'to do a man marking job on Robbo'. I had never done anything like this. Follow him everywhere, even to the toilet, I was told. My job was to not let Forest's best player play.

We were second favourites that wintry afternoon as Forest were riding high in the First Division. But there's never anything predictable about a Derby game. Throw in the FA Cup and a slag heap of a pitch and we had a chance.

Robbo was soon irritated about me stalking him. "F--- off, Millsy," he said, but it was all good banter. We laughed about the strange situation we found ourselves in, but it was serious stuff. I was even more determined to do my best. I was still a Forest player – well, I thought I was – but also a professional going about my business and I did it very well. Robbo never got a kick and got taken off midway through the second half which didn't happen very often. The tie swung in our favour when Archie Gemmill, who had his own score to settle with the Gaffer after the way he left the City Ground, netted a great free kick. It ended 2-0 to Derby, a great boost to everyone at the club and a job well done by me. Seven days later we were beaten 3-0 at Carlisle United!

Although Derby beat Chelsea in the cup and gave Manchester United a run for their money, as my wedding day approached, they still needed a couple of wins to escape from a very tight bottom of the division. Roy McFarland, who was working with Pete, asked me a couple of weeks before whether I would reschedule my wedding and stay a bit longer. Derby were prepared to compensate me financially, but the answer was no – that would have been more than my life's worth!

My stag do was in Stapleford at The Warren Arms pub where Gunny, Walshy, Donny, and I spent many hours socialising and became great pals with Ted and Stav. There was also a minibus load of family and friends from Northampton, including my two brothers, and Archie Gemmill also kindly came for a couple of drinks. From there we went on to Madisons in the city. Naturally it was a long night with plenty of booze, but I told everyone I was definitely going in for training.

What happened next sounded so corny, there was no way anyone at Derby was going to believe it – my car wouldn't start. Yes, honestly! Naturally they thought I was making an excuse and I waited for the repairman to come and eventually got there an hour or so late.

Then I realised why they wanted me in for training even though I was otherwise engaged on the Saturday. The lads got hold of me and plastered my body with boot polish. That was my farewell present from Derby County.

Our wedding took place on the Saturday at 3pm, at the same time Derby were kicking off against Sheffield Wednesday. It was a great day with Martyn as best man, Peter Ward's daughters as bridesmaids, and Kenny Hibbitt among the football folk. We had about 150 guests. Our schedule was very hectic as the next day we went on our honeymoon for five days to the Lake District, an area of the country we love so much. Then a couple of days later, it was America here we come. Little did we know what was going to happen next.

Sue and I were looking forward to the next part of our lives in America. It promised to be a magical start to married life – six months in a luxury apartment in an exciting part of the world, all before we got round to buying our first house. From a professional point of view, there was the challenge of playing again in front of huge crowds, and seeing if we could match or better our run to the Soccer Bowl final.

Looking back, the story of woe probably started well before we returned to Seattle as the club had parted company with Alan Hinton, who had arranged for me to go back a second time. In his place was Laurie Calloway, a name which didn't mean anything to me.

Seattle is the furthest you can fly to in America, so day one was always going to be a long one for us. We were met at the airport by Bobby Howe, Alan Hinton's former assistant and a familiar face. He drove us to the same apartment I had lived in in the previous year. Then came my first surprise - Bobby told me there was a friendly game that evening and I was playing.

I only had a couple of hours before Bobby drove me to the ground where I met my new teammates, before we boarded a ferry to continue the journey. I was knackered from the travelling but played the full 90 minutes in a 0-0 draw before missing in the shootout. Not the best of nights, but the reception I got from the manager shocked me. He was quite aggressive to everyone in the dressing room but singled me out for particular attention. "Don't think you are coming here to play like that – you can f--- off," he said. I couldn't believe my ears and was keen to speak with him after training the next day.

I said I'd been travelling almost a full day before playing in the game and wanted to know where I stood with him. Even then he wasn't too friendly. "I don't want you here if you're going to play like that," he said. Welcome back to America, Gary! This wasn't the best of starts with the new manager and it brought home that I was Alan Hinton's signing, not his. Nevertheless the best thing to do was work hard in training and get myself into the team.

I did well enough in the other friendly games to start the first couple of league games, before disaster struck in the third. We were playing Vancouver Whitecaps in front of a large crowd at the Kingdome when I took the ball past Dave Watson, the former England, Manchester City, and Sunderland defender. Next thing I knew I somersaulted and landed with both my legs in front of me and my right foot at a right angle. It was a horrific sight and I panicked straightaway. I'd never had a meaningful injury in my football career, but here I was laid out on the artificial pitch in a 100,000-seater stadium not knowing what was going to happen next. It was the most horrendous, and weirdest feeling of my entire life so far.

Peter Ward came over and looked away – that said it all. When footballers do that, you know it's serious. It's a good thing Sue was watching in the stadium. Had this happened the previous season, I would have been thousands of miles from home with the difficult task of keeping in touch with my loved ones. At least she knew the score from the beginning and was there to help. Morbid thoughts flashed through my mind. I was still only 21 years old and had experienced things in football most could only dream of. But was it all over so early in my career? It honestly felt like the end of my world.

The ambulance came onto the pitch and I was taken to hospital where I watched as surgeons put my leg back together and put it in a plaster. I was awake through it all, watching on a screen. I was in hospital for three or four days and needed a wheelchair when I got out.

The medical verdict was no football for a year, well beyond the end of my stay in Seattle. There were no guarantees I would ever get myself back to the same fitness levels again. I wanted to go back home as soon as possible. Yet, injured or not, I was Seattle's player and was told I was staying until September. It all felt very strange, but I had no choice and nobody contacted me from Forest to ask how I was.

At least Sue was there this time and able to help. It gave us some valuable social time together, a big bonus at the start of our married life. This was going to be an extended honeymoon, but not the one we expected. About a week after coming out of hospital, we were invited to a house party. I was sat in the wheelchair with my foot up, when someone innocently tickled me on the bottom of my foot. Boy did that make me jump, but I thought nothing about it. In bed that night it started to hurt more and more. I told Sue something was wrong and needed help.

Back in hospital, it was confirmed my tibia bone had come apart again and I needed a second operation. This time the surgeon had a different idea. He inserted a metal rod in the middle of my tibia stretching from knee to ankle. Thankfully I was given a general anaesthetic. I've still got the metal rod to this day.

With the club's permission, we booked a week away in the original Disneyland, Los Angeles, which was a dream for both of us. But watching the side play in the Kingdome without me was a difficult experience. Within a few weeks I came face-to-face with Dave Watson at the return game. To my amazement, he didn't ask me how I was or acknowledge me at all. I will add though that in 1991, when I was playing for Leicester City at Roker Park against Sunderland and he was co-commentating, he did apologise to me. It was a surreal moment seeing him in the corridor about eight years later. Don't get me wrong I never held any grudge against Dave, a footballer who had a great career. These things happen.

I had an issue to settle with Seattle. I went to see the manager as there was no sign of my second signing on fee coming my way. He said he knew nothing about it and wasn't prepared to help.

That was how it was left until Sue and I went to see Peter Ward and his family. The telephone rang and it was Alan Hinton. Wardy had a chat, then passed the phone over. I was polite, particularly because he was no longer manager of the club, but reminded him of the agreement. When he said he couldn't do anything, I pointed out that he was the one who had brought me back to America. Alan Hinton exploded. Maybe I touched a nerve, but he launched a volley of expletives in my direction. I never got my money.

It was during my second stint in Seattle after I had broken my leg that I got a phone call with the very sad news that Nan had died. I was struggling anyway after getting injured, but being thousands of miles away and unable to get to the funeral made things even harder. My Nan and Pap were very important people in my life, and I lost them both within eight months, with Pap passing away in January 1984. I still miss them both dearly.

My stay in America confirmed my view that Seattle is a beautiful place and we made some great friends there. Football-wise it was a nightmare, although I had fun meeting Joe Corrigan, the former Manchester City and England goalkeeper, who is a great character, and we enjoyed getting together again with Roger Davies and Steve Daley, as well as spending a lot of time with Wardy.

But clearly things weren't going well either on or off the field. Our season ended early without reaching the play offs and much worse news was to come as the players were called into the massive offices to be told Seattle Sounders were folding. You've never seen such a sight as the vultures descended, grabbing anything they could. I ended up with some personal photographs but was more interested in knowing our return flight tickets to England were paid for.

I was still a long way short of playing again when I reported back to the City Ground after nearly a year. The Gaffer asked about my injury and I told him it was a very bad one and wouldn't be fit for months. Next came a total shock. "Well, I'm not paying you," he said.

"But why?" I replied. "I'm your player."

"You might be our player, but I'm not paying you. You better have a chat with the PFA (Professional Footballers' Association)," he said.

Talk about another kick in the teeth! This was becoming a mystery and a nightmare. All I had looked forward to when signing a new deal at Forest was playing for them and, now after being packed off to Derby and Seattle (twice), they weren't going to pay me until I got myself back on the pitch.

I had no choice but to seek out Gordon Taylor at the PFA. I travelled by train to Manchester and explained my story. He listened and then organised a meeting with the Gaffer. The outcome was the PFA agreed to pay my monthly wages until I played my first game back at Forest! I didn't understand what was happening but went along with it. Later in my career I would have asked more questions than I did. Instead, Sue and I bought our first house in Gedling and I put every ounce of energy and determination into getting myself fit.

Almost from the moment I found out how serious the break was, something extra kicked in in my mind. I wouldn't say I had taken playing football for granted, but thought I had a long playing career in front of me. The leg break changed all that. In one moment, I saw my career almost snatched away and had to fight to get it back. My goal was to play professional football again at the highest level – and make myself an even better player.

Several of the Forest lads went out of their way to help and encourage me. Paul Hart showed me the trick of putting on a bin bag with holes for the head and arms, to get a sweat on and keep my weight down, and goalkeeper Steve Sutton paid me the compliment of saying he had never seen anyone work so hard to get fit.

By Christmas and New Year, I was turning the corner. I knew I could get back on the pitch before the forecast year was up. My first game of football was a youth game. I can't describe the feeling of going into a few tackles. It was fantastic. No time though to rest on my laurels. My contract was up at the end of June and I hadn't played for the first team for nearly two seasons. I needed to show what I could do -and fast.

Two or three reserve games told me all was well physically, and I was in the squad for the away leg of our UEFA Cup quarter final against Austrian side Sturm Graz. Forest were doing well in the First Division, but Europe was our big chance of silverware after a brilliant victory over Celtic at Parkhead in the previous round.

The Gaffer took us for a walk, as he liked to do, when suddenly we noticed him doing something very strange. He was punching a tree like a boxer. The lads were laughing thinking he had really lost the plot this time. "Look you ignorant lot," he said. "Form a circle and start punching the tree. This is what you call a punch tree!" So that's what we did! One by one we punched the tree until he called stop.

On the day of the match, the Gaffer pulled me aside after training and told me he had a dilemma. "You know that agreement with the PFA that they pay you until we play you – well, I want to play you tonight, but I don't want to pay you." I could hardly believe what I was hearing as he went on: "The decision is up to you. If you want to play, the PFA will still pay you!"

"Gaffer, you are kidding me," I replied. "I have worked, worked, and worked so hard for this moment, and I'm ready to play and you don't want to pay me!"

I decided not to play out of principle as the club was going back on our agreement – yet another low blow. Fortunately the lads battled through to the semi final and this time I played both legs of that infamous tie against Anderlecht with the PFA still paying my wages. Two late Steve Hodge goals earned us a 2-0 victory in the first leg at the City Ground, so we travelled to Brussels in a confident mood. Nobody who supports Forest, and was also around in those days, will ever forget what happened next – and it lives with me forever.

We were on the receiving end of several disgraceful decisions from the referee that night, as well as being under a lot of pressure from the home side. The latter wasn't a great problem as we thrived on soaking up pressure from our opponents and hitting them hard when we had the chance. Realistically, we knew an away goal would almost certainly be enough to get through to the final.

With Anderlecht leading 1-0 on the night, an awful penalty was awarded against our full back Kenny Swain. I was near enough to see their player was never touched. We knew we had to score when they went 3-0 up, and I took the last minute corner that is still talked about today. Everyone knows there was no foul by Paul Hart as he rose and sent a fantastic header into the net. It was a goal, pure and simple, and would have won the tie. But somehow the referee disallowed it. All the players and the Gaffer were numb in the dressing room. Hartie is a big man and even he was in tears. We thought we had been done by a terrible mistake – we didn't know the half of it!

When it came out officially years later that the referee had been bribed, it didn't help. Even the idea of being compensated financially didn't mean much. What I and the other Forest players lost that night wasn't so much money, but the guarantee of another medal. To me, that was the second European medal I missed out on.

Watching Spurs in a final they eventually won on penalties was sheer torture. I knew it should have been us on that pitch. Of all the Forest players, I felt that blow as badly as anyone. I know the effort and sacrifice I put into getting myself playing again to try and win a trophy. That chance was taken away because a referee, who has since lost his life, didn't have the balls to do the right thing. Even now in 2021 when I watch the Europa League, today's version of the UEFA Cup, it still hurts knowing we could have won it.

CHAPTER 5
THE GAFFER'S YOUNG MEN AND A SURPRISE MOVE

By JOHN BARNWELL, former Notts County manager

RIVALRIES being what they are, it was a big move for Gary Mills to come across the Trent from Forest.

Gary was perfect for the balance of my side. I liked one of my full backs to 'push on', the other to stay at home. Gary could bomb up and down the right side all day.

I had one very big victory over Brian Clough with Wolves at Wembley; I also got the better of him at the transfer tribunal when we signed Gary.

He soon won over Notts fans because of his attitude. They recognise when someone works very hard for the team and Gary did that. You can't turn attitude on and off. What he did in training was reflected in the games.

I worked with a lot of footballers over my 50 years plus in the game and Gary Mills is one of those to whom the label 'best professional' is appropriate.

He rarely missed training, he was thoughtful and would question what I asked him to do, but he would go out on the pitch and do it – and put the team above himself.

I think we were the best footballing team in the division with the likes of Gary Mills, Garry Birtles, Geoff Pike and Adrian Thorpe in the side, but we had a couple of injuries late on and missed out on promotion in the play offs. That's football . . . .

*****

ANYONE thinking Forest's season ended with that controversial defeat is way off the mark. The Gaffer would never have allowed that and, as for me, my mini season was only just beginning!

Gutted as I was at missing out on another European final, getting into Forest's First Division side as we ended the season strongly was important after the strangest three years of my football career. I was involved in games against Stoke and Leicester, followed by wins against Watford, West Ham, and Manchester United to give the Gaffer the message that I was back at Forest.

Gunny, whose deal was also up, waited outside the Gaffer's office with me. We both had butterflies. Gunny was adamant he was not going to sign a new deal. He had been around for years – even longer than me – and needed to be playing first team football week in, week out. After being a regular the previous two seasons, he hadn't featured much in 1983/84. What happened next still makes me smile. "Gunny, get your arse in here," roared the Gaffer.

A few minutes later, out walked Gunny. "I've just signed a two-year deal on the same money," he said. You couldn't make this up. The Gaffer also had good news for me. He gave me another three-year deal on improved terms, but it was what he said that meant just as much. He said I had worked so hard; he was very pleased and no one could have deserved the new deal more. Hearing that was fantastic. I felt wanted, with a very big three years ahead of me.

I rate the three years that followed as the best years of my Forest career. We may not have been as successful as in the unbelievable seasons that had gone before, but I produced the best football of my career from 1984 to 1987 and particularly in 1986/7, which proved to be my last season at Forest.

It all started with a brilliant end-of-season tour to Australia in 1984. Sue was pregnant with our first child which made the timing interesting, but it was still a memorable three weeks. The first surprise was getting on the bus in Nottingham and the Gaffer saying: "Have a nice time, I will see you in Melbourne." The Gaffer wasn't going with us and none of us believed his vow he would be flying out separately.

It proved a great trip, probably our best ever, even minus the Gaffer, as we went to Perth, Sydney, Melbourne and Adelaide. There was some football, including a game against Manchester United in Sydney and two matches against the Australian national team live on TV, and time for socialising too. We had travelled for what seemed like days when we got to Perth and everyone was knackered. Ron Fenton, the Gaffer's assistant, organised a bus trip around Perth, but whilst the tour guide did his best to interest us in all the sights, everyone was asleep. The only words I remember hearing were when Ronnie said: "Off the bus lads, we are going for a drink!" That woke us all up! We perked up so much most of us even defied Ronnie's orders to get to bed early and had a good night out in Perth.

We discovered indoor cricket which proved a great laugh as Jim McInally, good full back though he was, showed his talents didn't extend to bowling, and there was the fun of Hodgy losing all of his cases. We had so many trips, here, there, and everywhere with Forest, and usually enjoyed ourselves when the hard work was over.

Walshy and I came across two very familiar faces at our hotel in Brisbane. When the lift doors opened, there was the famous ice dance duo Jayne Torvill and Christopher Dean. Being a little braver after a few drinks, we introduced ourselves as also being from Nottingham and they invited the whole squad to see their show and meet them afterwards. That was another great experience.

There was another European adventure to look forward to in the UEFA Cup after we finished third the previous season. It was always going to be an edgy time for me as Sue was booked into hospital for a caesarean on October 4 for the birth of our son, the day after we played the second leg of our first round UEFA Cup tie in Bruges. But my pre-match sickness couldn't be blamed on nerves or thinking about what my wife was going through. It was more to do with the horse meat we ate in Belgium!

The football didn't go well either. After a scoreless game at the City Ground, we were dumped out of the cup 1-0. That was disappointing enough, but I was in an even worse state being sick again. When I got to the hospital for the birth, I was in a mess. Sue and I have a good laugh about it now. There she was giving birth and the medical staff were pampering me. I was sick again in the hospital toilet but was there for the big moment. The birth of our son Ryan was incredible. "It's me!" I cried when I looked at him for the first time. He was the very image. I lost 10lbs in weight in five days, but that was soon forgotten as we started our new life as a family.

December 1984 saw two memorable Forest matches as we came back from 2-0 down to beat both Manchester United and Villa 3-2 at the City Ground, with Johnny Metgod working his magic with free kicks. But, for me, they bring back contrasting memories. The United game is the happy one. I scored the goal to equalise at 2-2, before going back to Northampton in the evening and enjoying the surreal moment of watching my goal in a bar on *Match of the Day* with friends. But I was injured again when Villa came to town.

We flew to the Middle East in midweek, returning on the Friday, before a trip to Goodison Park to face Everton the following afternoon. We went straight from the airport to Haydock Park Hotel where, after a bite to eat, the Gaffer led us on one of his customary walks. Suddenly he walked up a driveway and told us to sing 'We Wish You A Merry Christmas' when the door opened. We were wondering what this was all about when Duncan McKenzie, the former Forest and Everton player, appeared. He was delighted and invited us all inside, but the Gaffer said we were busy. That meant going back to the hotel and having a few drinks until gone midnight, when we scrambled into our beds.

Next day was a total disaster for Forest but even more so for me. I was playing right back and, as I cleared the ball up the line, Everton striker Graeme Sharp came across to make a block. I collapsed in agony close to our dugout. "F---ing get up!" was the familiar cry from the Gaffer. But I couldn't. I was in agony and had to be stretchered off. I was laid out on the table in the dressing room when Chris Fairclough came in about five minutes later, saying: "I got him for you!" He was sent off for his tackle on Graeme Sharp, and we lost 5-0.

I'd broken my left leg this time. Not as bad as the injury in America, but still a big setback. I'd broken my fibula - but not my tibia - and would be out for two to three months. The only consolation was the surgeon could now remove the metal pin from my right leg whilst fixing the other one.

It was devastating so soon after getting myself fit, but I managed to get myself back into the team by March 20th for a home game against Sheffield Wednesday. Despite the layoff, I ended up playing 31 games that season and also scored in three successive games. The first was a particular thrill for a former

Arsenal fan as I put one past John Lukic in a 1-1 draw at Highbury. Viv Anderson was in the Gunners side. The other goals came in victories over Coventry and Luton.

I also played in the return game against Everton at the City Ground in May, on the day of the tragic Bradford fire. The Gaffer went into the Everton dugout before kick off with a special message for Graeme. "Pity you aren't playing –my son Nigel was going to break your leg today!"

Then he wished Sharpy all the best for the forthcoming European Cup Winners' Cup final, in which Howard Kendall's side beat Rapid Vienna. We got some revenge as a Gaz Birtles' goal gave us victory over the league champions and ended their long unbeaten run. Again I had no ill feelings about Sharpy. Just my bad luck that lightning struck twice!

A few months later, the Gaffer showed his more human side when, with Valley Parade out of action, we played Bradford City at Odsal on a cold night in the League Cup.

Mum and Dad went to watch and the Gaffer noticed me giving them both a kiss in the car park afterwards. I used to kiss both my Dad and Pap because they meant everything to me.

The Gaffer was sat near the front of the bus and said: "Mr and Mrs Mills, come onto my bus." They weren't keen because it was already 10pm and they had a long trip home but the Gaffer insisted. Then he told me: "Well done for giving your Dad a kiss. that's a lovely thing to do. Now give them a glass of whiskey to warm them up." Things like that mean a lot and tell you what kind of man he was.

My last two seasons at Forest saw the rapid development of a team that would probably be remembered even more fondly by the fans, had we not had the incredible European and domestic success a few years earlier.

The critics said the Gaffer was never able to repeat that kind of success, but they missed the point. His team from the late 1980s was successful by almost any other standard, twice finishing third in the First Division, winning two League Cups, reaching the FA Cup final, and claiming other domestic trophies. And a lot of that success came through the very difficult process of bringing young players through the ranks rather than splashing the cash.

Even the biggest name of all in that Forest team, skipper Stuart Pearce, was brought in for relative peanuts as the lightweight in a £300,000 deal with fellow Coventry player Ian Butterworth. It was Ian and his wife that I got to know better in my time at the City Ground, but Butters became one of those players who didn't quite make it into Forest's brilliant young side.

Alongside Psycho, a top, top player, Des Walker, Chris Fairclough and, later Terry Wilson and Gary Fleming, all developed into fine defenders. Again Des benefited from being at a club brave enough to give him his chance at an early age. He became better and better, developing into a world class defender and a lot of that was due to the way he was nurtured at Forest.

It wasn't all about young players, of course. Ian 'Bomber' Bowyer had almost become the father figure of the club and no praise is high enough for his contribution to Forest. In my opinion, he was one of Forest's greats and always will be.

'Bomber' scored countless vital goals for Forest and was also a great, great professional who commanded respect for who he was, as well as his ability. It was vital to have experienced players like him around who would certainly let others know when they weren't doing their jobs.

There was also Hartie and Kenny Swain in the early part of that era, who had been there and done everything, whilst the likes of Hodgy and me were joining the ranks of the more established players in the squad.

Ours remained both a happy and a confident dressing room, right up to the time I left Forest, and it was a huge tribute to the Gaffer and his team that they finished in the top half of the First Division every year but one in the 1980s.

I made 18 appearances in 1985/6, but rate my final year as my best when I played 33 times. Things went so well, I honestly thought I had a chance of being Forest's Player of the Year for the first time. That made what happened next more confusing.

In February the Gaffer told me Glasgow Rangers were interested in signing me. I knew I was coming towards the end of my contract and with Sue heavily pregnant – our daughter Jenna was born on March 3 – I needed to secure my future. But this was something totally out of the blue. I'd never been told of interest from other clubs – aside from Seattle and Derby – so I needed time to think.

A phone call to former Forest teammate Chris Woods influenced me. "Get your arse up here, Millsy, this is a fantastic club," he said. England internationals Terry Butcher and Trevor Steven were already there, as manager Graeme Souness was building a very strong side.

I made my mind up – I was interested in the move. I found the Gaffer having a bath in the referee's room and told him the news. "Leave it with me, we'll f---ing sort it out," he said. Leaving was a daunting thought as Nottingham was home and Forest was my club. Big things were happening in my family life and my next move, whether staying at the City Ground or going elsewhere, had to be right.

The papers were full of talk that a £150,000 fee had been agreed between the two clubs and I was on my way. In fact, all I had done was agree to travel to Glasgow for talks with Graeme Souness.

I was due to drive up on the Monday, and was in the Forest side on the Saturday at Queen's Park Rangers. We stopped at Luton, just off the M1, on the Friday and I had a long chat in the bar after dinner with the Gaffer. He asked whether I was sure about the move and I said I had no intention of leaving until he said he was willing to let me go. We sat for a couple of hours drinking a few pints, and it was quite emotional. He said it had been a pleasure working with me, we had enjoyed some good times and I wouldn't get the chance to drink with my new gaffer in Scotland like this. What he said was lovely, but also a little sad.

I played at Loftus Road and was all packed ready for the trip when I got a call from Ronnie Fenton on the Sunday. "Hi Gary, the deal's off, you will be back in training in the morning. The Gaffer says make sure you're not late!" That was it. No explanation. I knocked on the Gaffer's door in the morning. "Deal's off, just get f---ing training. You are f---ing staying here, son!" I still had no clue what had gone on, so I just went along with it.

Throughout my time at Forest we had a lot of short breaks abroad, with Malta and Cala Millor being our favourite venues. This was all part of what I now put down as the forward thinking and genius of the Gaffer. There's constant chat these days about players being tired – and I get that to a certain extent – but the way the Gaffer rested players was not by rotating or leaving them out of important games, but by giving us all plenty of time off. Today the players are in virtually every day and I think that's self-defeating because the tiredness they talk about isn't just physical, it's mental.

The last thing footballers need is to go over and over the mistakes they made in the last game. Time to breathe, relax, and put our feet up was the Gaffer's way of ensuring we were ready for battle.

The many trips did have one complication – wives and girlfriends weren't always happy. Often, we didn't know until the day before we were flying off somewhere, and the first indication was a bunch of flowers arriving through the door for our partners.

There were also the strange incidents, such as what happened to our new signing Paul Wilkinson after he made his debut in a 2-0 defeat at Old Trafford. Wilko is probably best remembered by Forest fans for his thunderous long range goal against Arsenal in the FA Cup, but it's a different story in the dressing room. Wilko kept himself to himself on the coach trip to Heathrow, whilst most of us were winding down with a drink or two. We were generally quite merry as we were going through security at the airport, when suddenly the cry went out 'Where's Wilko?' We then found that he had collapsed. The Gaffer's first thought was that he had been drinking, but that wasn't the case.

Also towards the end of my career at Forest, I played my first and only game at Plough Lane against the 'Crazy Gang'. That was an eye opener. Now, having been a Non-League manager for many years, I'd compare the facilities at Wimbledon to a lower league ground. It was remarkable we played there in the First Division. Wimbledon, with John Fashanu up front and Vinny Jones and Dennis Wise in midfield, were intimidatory. That was their way, the way they played, and they were successful. It wasn't mine.

I took the collapse of the Rangers deal as a hint Forest still wanted me, but my future was up in the air come the end of the season. Talking to the Gaffer about a new deal wasn't as straightforward as before. I knew what I wanted now instead of just accepting what was put in front of me. My form merited a wage increase, so I asked for an extra £50 a week. And I still wanted my 1979 European Cup medal! It was increasingly frustrating asking the Gaffer the same question again and again over the years, and his answers became more and more vague. At first, he promised me the medal, but by then he was irritated whenever I brought it up.

I had three or four meetings with the Gaffer. A couple lasted half an hour, the others a couple of minutes. The last time he was in one of his moods. There was no budging on the wage issue and he rounded off by saying: "I f---ing told you I would get your medal, now get out of my office!" That was when I knew I was finished at Forest. I was done. It was a heartbreaking way to end a fantastic part of my life, but I couldn't back down. It makes me emotional even now thinking about it. I needed and deserved to feel valued.

I couldn't understand the Gaffer's reluctance to see me right. The moment I left his office I wanted out of the place as quickly as possible. After training, I sprinted up the side of the Trent to get to the ground first. The door was locked and the only way in was climbing onto a car bonnet and forcing the window open. Without bothering to have a shower, I dropped off my training kit, picked up my bag, climbed out of the same window, and drove home.

Ronnie Fenton rang me later about arrangements for our pre-season trip the following day. "I'm not going – I'm not signing," I told him. He said something on the lines of 'don't be stupid' but I was never going to change my mind. So that was it. I didn't have a club or an agent, and had no idea about my next move.

I had a magnificent time at Nottingham Forest. So many special memories. And it all came to an end over £50 and a 1979 European Cup medal. Leaving Forest was the most difficult decision of my football career. With a three-year contract on the table, I didn't take that decision lightly. I shed a few tears and tortured myself over whether I'd done the right thing. But, looking back on it now, I have no regrets.

People questioned my ambition when I then moved down two divisions to play with Notts County. But I believed in what Notts were trying to do. I went to a club who wanted to get into the top league, where I still wanted to play. There was interest from Sheffield United, another massive club within travelling distance from Nottingham. I went to speak with manager Billy McEwan, but it didn't feel right. I also took a call from French club Brest but wasn't convinced about that either.

Then Gaz Birtles rang out of the blue. He had moved across the Trent to join Notts along with Paul Hart, who was player coach. I said dropping down two divisions had never entered my head. Gaz said he had been asked to ring and that Notts, under new manager John Barnwell, had an exciting project and wouldn't be in the Third Division for long. That was followed by the manager asking to come and see me and I liked him straightaway. What a lovely man!

John Barnwell told me more about County's plans and I spoke with chairman Derek Pavis, who had also swapped Nottingham clubs. Although Notts may not have been my initial choice, the move did have some things going for it – I felt wanted, could still live in Nottingham, and would be playing with a couple of players I felt closest to at Forest. Nevertheless, I asked for a few days to think it over.

Then I got back in touch with John Barnwell and he invited me down to Meadow Lane. I dressed in a suit, collar, and tie out of respect. I told him I was keen on principle to sign for Notts and they were willing to pay me the wage I was denied at Forest. I'm a simple man in the best sense and I was very excited about joining them. When I signed the contract, I found out something about Derek Pavis when shaking on the deal– he had the biggest hands I have ever seen. I got on extremely well with Mr Pavis who said: "I'm so pleased you have signed for us, my lad." 'My lad' was his catch phrase for everyone he met!

I made my debut in an eventful 4-4 draw against Wigan before the tribunal fixed the transfer fee. I overheard Derek Pavis and Brian Clough talking. Mr Pavis told him there was more entertainment at Meadow Lane on Saturday than there had been at the City Ground recently. The Gaffer typically replied on the lines that he was sure Derek was right, and wished him a nice day.

There was a great squad and sense of togetherness at Notts. I felt happy and at home. I was happy with my football, enjoyed going into work every day, and had a good relationship with the fans. There was one more important thing to settle – the fee. The two clubs couldn't agree so we went to a tribunal with Forest asking for £200,000 and Notts offering £50,000. My old gaffer gave evidence. I was quizzed about why I wanted to join Notts, and I think they were surprised when I told them the Magpies were offering me more money than Forest! The tribunal agreed a fee of £57,500 which pleased the chairman. "We've had a good result today, my lad," he said. My old gaffer gave me an 'alright son' and that was about it.

I was very happy at Notts and still don't know how we didn't get a promotion whilst I was there. We were a good team with former West Ham player Geoff Pike as captain, Gaz or sometimes Andy Gray, the former Scotland legend, at centre half, and Charlie McParland knocking in the goals.

Whatever Notts fans thought when I joined from Forest, I soon won them over. They could see what type of man and player I was and I was thrilled to be voted player of the season. That was always a big honour in my book. I valued winning it at Notts and Leicester. As a manager, I tell the lads at the start of the season that one of them is going to be player of the season come May – just make sure it's you.

There was good banter at Notts. Gaz got the same sort of stick for his dress sense as he had at Forest, as Adrian Thorpe, one of the pranksters, left a pair of his leather trousers three quarters of the way up a floodlight pylon. Another of Gaz's fashions was wearing winklepicker shoes with his tracksuit as he refused to wear trainers.

We had a young Tommy Johnson, later to become a Notts hero, in the squad. Then, he was a young lad who looked about nine stones wet through. Derek Pavis, who liked coming down to the training ground, was soon on his case. He looked at the youngster and said: "Now, what are we going to do about you, my lad?" From then on, he brought him steak and a box of vegetables to training every week and would ask Tommy if he had eaten his veg.

I liked the way John Barnwell played his football, I liked the man and still know him today. One day John made me laugh. He took me with him to the new training ground at Stoke Bardolph and asked me to do a headstand. I couldn't believe it, but I got on my hands and did it. "That's one of the best headstands I have seen in my life," he said. He was still talking about it when we got back with the rest of the lads.

The only missing piece was promotion – otherwise it was a really enjoyable season, in which I played every minute of all 60 matches. We narrowly missed out on going up automatically, and were beaten in the play off semi final by Walsall who did the damage by winning 3-1 at Meadow Lane. David Kelly, later a teammate at Leicester, scored a couple of goals that day.

The team suffered a bit of a hangover the following season when we made a poor start, leading to John Barnwell's dismissal halfway through the campaign. That was shortly after I had a surprise visit at home. It was in late November and Derek Pavis' son was at my door. He said he hadn't been sent by his Dad but heard John Barnwell had lost the dressing room and asked whether it was true. I was shocked by this approach and told him to leave. I never experienced anything like that in my career and wasn't comfortable. He had come to the wrong place and the wrong person. The answer though was that we were still playing for John Barnwell – for some reason it just wasn't working.

Two or three weeks later John got the sack. He knew he was under pressure, but it was an emotional moment when I saw him walk through the door for the last time. I followed him out and said I was devastated to see him go and thanked him for everything he had done for me at Notts. This was the first time I'd seen a manager sacked – apart from when I was on loan at Derby – and I could see the hurt on his face. Today, having experienced that myself, I know exactly how he was feeling.

We knew we were getting a new manager but didn't know who. Then in walked Neil Warnock. We didn't know too much about Neil Warnock back then as he was in the early stages of his long managerial career. It soon became clear though that he had different ideas than John Barnwell on how to play the game.

As a full back, I felt comfortable getting on the ball, perhaps moving into space or picking a pass. That's the way I was brought up. Neil Warnock didn't want me to do that. He insisted I played the ball over the head of the opposing full back, so we could then press them back in their final third and try to win a free kick or a throw in.

Neil was a chiropodist. He did my feet, as he did for the other players, on the treatment table in the dressing room. On the Friday night of Neil's first away game, he invited each of us in turn into his hotel room and quizzed us on who we thought wasn't pulling their weight. Again, I didn't give a positive answer to a question I didn't think I should have been asked. All I said was that I would always give everything. When a team isn't winning, everyone, including the media and the fans, look for reasons. I don't hold that against Neil, but it isn't the way I go about it.

It didn't come as a surprise when the new manager asked me to stay behind for a chat after training. We were in his car when he said he didn't think I was his type of player. I had no problem with that. I agreed. To make things clear for Notts fans, I was very happy at the club. Although results weren't going as well as we all hoped, I was playing well and it was a great place to be.

West Brom came in and I took Sue with me to meet manager Brian Talbot for talks. They offered Notts £300,000 and me a contract which would have been the best money of my career. He showed me around the ground and the dressing rooms. We had booked a hotel near the ground – the one we stayed in when playing at The Hawthorns - and we went back there for lunch to think about what had been said. The deal was great, but somehow, I still didn't feel right about it. Sue made a tongue-in-cheek comment that she didn't like the idea of moving to the Birmingham area because our children would end up talking in a West Midlands accent. She even said so to Brian Talbot and, believe it or not, it made the headlines of the local paper.

CHAPTER 6
REACHING MY PEAK
WITH THE FOXES

SOON afterwards, Leicester City manager David Pleat phoned to say he had heard I'd been talking to West Brom but would love me to sign for The Foxes. I knew this was the club for me - half an hour down the road and a big football club. Even the fact they were struggling in the Second Division was no problem – this was still a step up from the Third.

Notts fans knew a night game at Meadow Lane was likely to be my last. David Pleat said he was coming and would talk with me afterwards but, as far as I knew, a deal had already been agreed with the Magpies. I had a good game, and we were winning comfortably when the manager pulled me off in the 85th minute, allowing me to get a very good ovation from the fans. That was a really nice gesture, highlighting there was never a problem between me and Neil Warnock.

Afterwards in the boardroom, Derek Pavis invited both me and Sue, along with David Pleat, back to his house. There he pulled me aside into another room and made it clear he still wanted me to stay. We chatted until about 3am or 4am and I told him that, although I was happy at the club, the manager and I believed it was mutually beneficial for me to move on.

That came true as Notts got Phil Turner in the swap deal, in which I was valued at £300,000, more than five times what they had paid for me. Phil, who still lives in the same village as me, contributed to County's subsequent rise whilst I played what I consider to be my best football during five seasons at Filbert Street. We both helped our new clubs to eventually get back into the topflight of English football.

It was a great pleasure when Neil Warnock invited me back to Meadow Lane to celebrate Notts' initial promotion to Division Two – this doesn't happen with many players, so it was a great gesture by Neil.

My Leicester deal was nothing near as good as WBA, but it felt right and I agreed to it the next day. I joined a side that had potential with very good players such as Gary McAllister, Mike Newell, Martin Hodge, and Steve Walsh.

David Pleat's training methods were completely different from anything I had experienced before. The boss played 'follow the leader games' and was obsessed with passing the ball, even though some players found that very difficult.

His eccentricities included blowing a whistle during training and firing out random questions, normally to Steve Walsh, such as "what is the capital of Sweden?"

Walshy would reply: "Oslo, gaffer!"

Then the gaffer would say "you stupid boy, it's Stockholm!" It was like a scene between Captain Mainwaring and Pike in *Dad's Army*.

Being at Leicester City was a personal challenge which I relished. Results had been poor and fans were getting on the manager's back, yet the atmosphere around the club was great and the dressing room was ok.

The gaffer shared my liking for health clubs. When he booked us into Barnsdale Country Club in Rutland for training and relaxation, I thrived on it. I've been going to Barnsdale ever since – it is beautiful. In fact, I fell in love with it so much, I now take teams I manage there for pre-season training.

Another health place the gaffer took us to was Hendon Hall and it was there that my love for saunas led to a wonderful chance meeting. I was sat all on my own when in walked boxing legend Frank Bruno. I couldn't believe my eyes. Frank was a national hero and probably my favourite sportsperson at the time. I explained I was there with Leicester City and we then had a wonderful conversation. He asked about our fitness training and couldn't believe how little we did. We must have been in there for a good hour chatting away. It was lovely and a real bonus meeting him – something I will never forget.

Also at Hendon Hall, David Pleat took us for a relaxation course. We were concentrating on our breathing and following the soothing instructions, when the spell was broken by the sound of the manager snoring loudly. Left back Tony Spearing, who was a comedian, started taking the mickey and we fell about laughing.

Another good moment with Tony was when we were about to run out to face West Brom at The Hawthorns. David Pleat was standing right next to a huge clock in the away dressing room when Spearo asked him the time. When he answered, 'six minutes to three' we couldn't stop ourselves laughing when Pleaty said 'you stupid boy, Spearing'. Another Dad's Army moment!

Soon after I joined, we went to play at Plymouth Argyle. We went down on the Friday night and the manager said we would be welcoming a new signing. Even when we got to the hotel, he didn't tell us who it was. I looked on the guest list as I was due to be rooming with the new man. I waited for him to arrive then the door opened and in waltzed Mick Kennedy, from Portsmouth. I knew a little about him because Pompey had some hard players, and he was one of them. I was lying on the bed as he introduced himself by pulling out a six pack of beers and 20 cigarettes from his bag and said: "That's me! If you don't like it, room with someone else!"

That was quite an introduction, but not as good as the one in the dressing room the next day. The bell had just gone at 2.55pm when Mick stood up and ranted "Right, do you want to f---ng win?" before headbutting, punching and kicking the wall shouting 'devilment'. I couldn't believe it – Gary McAllister and I couldn't stop laughing. I generally got on very well with Mick afterwards, but he scared the life out of our new signing Kevin 'the Rooster' Russell on our summer tour of Sweden. I have been on many tours in different countries but it's right what they say about Sweden – it's a very quiet place with not too many places of entertainment.

There were no pubs anywhere, so we settled for a pizza bar to have a couple of beers – or, in Mick's case, a few more. 'Rooster' ran into the room I was sharing with Mick, shouting 'hide me, Mick Kennedy is trying to take me to the pizza bar'. He'd been there a few times already and had had enough. He hid in the wardrobe when Mick made his entrance. "Where's that bloody Rooster? He said he was coming out with me." I denied all knowledge but, as Mick was leaving, he heard noise coming from the wardrobe and our cover was blown. Mick then got Rooster by the scruff of the neck and dragged him out.

The manager confused me at times. After we had been thrashed 6-0 in a midweek game at Middlesbrough, he said 'well done' to some players and picked up on aspects of play he liked. Goalkeeper Martin Hodge stood up angrily and asked what he was talking about when we had just got hammered. But that was David Pleat, a calm man, who didn't quite instil the discipline we needed. Some players weren't doing their jobs well and, it's fair to say, not playing for the manager.

One of the great characters in that Leicester side was Ally Mauchlen. We called him the 'mad man' or 'mad dog' because he was capable of anything, as well as being a very good footballer. He didn't let us down with a particular party trick when the lads had our Christmas drink. We began the binge with two or three pints in the first pub, and were a bit bewildered when Ally walked out with a framed picture tucked under his arm. This was a seriously big picture which he then carried from pub to pub for the rest of the day. We must have set off about 1pm before returning to the first pub about eight hours later where Ally made a grand entrance by walking in and hanging the picture back on its hook on the wall – like I said, 'mad dog'.

We brought in some good players including Terry Fenwick, who played for David Pleat at Spurs, and a young Kevin Campbell on loan from Arsenal who banged in a few goals. But we couldn't seem to get on a consistent run. The manager was fascinated with Brian Clough. He often asked me what my former boss would do in a particular situation. "Give us three days off!" I said.

"No, no, be serious," he said.

I replied "I am being serious." I'm still not sure whether he believed me.

Walshy was also interested in knowing more about Brian Clough, and found out more for himself when he and I attended a referees' meeting at Filbert Street. The meeting was for managers and captains of Midlands clubs and all of a sudden, my old gaffer walked in. He stayed quiet for almost the whole meeting, at which the conduct of players with referees was being discussed, when he stood up unannounced and said: "Gentlemen, I'm very sorry, I can't stay any longer because I've got to take my wife Barbara shopping – but I would just like to say, you're all a f---ing disgrace". Everyone else in the room was shocked but laughing – except, of course, for me.

We also had some fun at the expense of Darren Williams, one of the younger lads. He noticed that Rooster travelled a long way for training and was getting cash for his mileage. So, we kidded Darren he could be due some more money. Darren was a fitness fanatic and we said he should ask the manager to pay for his pints of Guinness, which were full of iron, and his raw eggs. He realised he'd been had after knocking on the manager's door and getting a short shrift.

My first full season at Leicester, 1989-90, went well for me personally, and although I missed a few weeks with an achilles injury, I became player of the year and also scored their goal of the season. I picked up the ball in our own half against Watford at Filbert Street, beat four players, and let fly with a left foot shot from the edge of the box that flew past David James, who later became England's goalkeeper. I got another good one – a half volley to open the scoring in the final game of the season against Sheffield United when they won 5-2 to clinch promotion. Helping us beat Leeds 4-3 at Filbert Street on my birthday was another good memory.

The following season was one Leicester City fans will never forget as we survived the dreaded drop to the Third Division on the last day. The campaign was a problem from the start. We sold Gary McAllister, probably our best player, and bringing in loan players wasn't working. I was sad to see David Pleat go but his sacking was inevitable, and the players were quick to voice their opinions. We had a lot of respect for Gordon Lee, the former Everton manager, and David Pleat's assistant, and we got our way. Gordon Lee was brought in as caretaker for the rest of the season.

I probably didn't realise it, but that was a very stressful time for him. I doubt he got much sleep as we hovered in or around the relegation zone for the next four months, but he never communicated that stress to us. He made it a relaxed atmosphere, playing five-a-side, and keeping it simple. He brought laughter back to the training ground and there was no doubt we were playing for him.

Results were mixed. Scoring a header in a 2-0 win over Notts at Meadow Lane was special for me, but there were plenty of difficult days too. Finally, after picking up just a single point in our previous three games, we went into the last match against Oxford United at Filbert Street with our destiny out of our hands.

That was pressure. You could feel the anxiety everywhere. The fight we had in that side was incredible, but we knew that even a win might not be enough. Nearest rivals West Brom knew victory at Bristol Rovers would keep them up whatever happened to us. Tony James gave us an early lead and we dominated the match. Still, it was always on a knife edge at 1-0, never mind what was happening at Bristol. Being a wide player, endless scores were shouted at me. I swear I heard the lot from West Brom winning to losing.

We knew Rovers had a player sent off very early on, giving West Brom plenty of time to make it count. When the whistle went and we had won 1-0, we were desperate to know the real score at Bristol.

The home side took the lead towards the end only for West Brom to level in injury time. Eventually we got the good news the game had finished 1-1 and we were safe.

What a weird feeling! We hadn't won a league or a cup, in fact we hadn't had a good season at all, but none of that mattered. I shared tears of sheer emotion with Alan Birchenall in the tunnel. It was an incredible feeling. I was so pleased for Gordon. He had done everything he could to guarantee we would give him 100 per cent and it paid off. We were even more pleased when a couple of days later he told us to get our passports as we were off to Portugal for a week to celebrate. And celebrate we did!

I don't think Gordon Lee was ever getting the job permanently – I don't think he wanted it anyway. But hiring Brian Little in the summer, who brought Allan Evans and John Gregory to work with him, proved an inspired move.

My first two full seasons were difficult for the team, but I knew I was playing well and loving life at Leicester City and now our fortunes started to turn around. Brian Little was a good manager and introduced the discipline which, without doubt, was missing from David Pleat's dressing room. Fines for not wearing flip flops in the shower or leaving kit on the training field might seem insignificant but were all part and parcel of us being more professional and doing the right things.

As Brian Little improved things on the field, major changes were happening behind the scenes. Barrie Pierpoint, who became chief executive, breezed into Filbert Street, bringing with him a whole new mindset. The big man was responsible for a lot of innovations that improved Leicester City FC including Family Night Football.

Barrie was a real character who somehow managed to wear a different coloured spectacles every day and generally brought much-needed energy to the club.

I was personally grateful because he was responsible for me getting my first ever sponsored car. In return, he knew I was one of the players who would help out when he needed something doing in the community. We remain good friends to this day.

I played every minute of all 61 games that season, a minor miracle in the circumstances. It was no thanks to Ian Wright after an incident in a League Cup tie at Filbert Street. The future Gunners legend, making his debut after signing from Crystal Palace, left his mark on me. I was one of two defenders standing on the halfway line marking Wrighty as we had a corner. As we took the kick, Wright stamped on my foot – obviously one of his tricks.

I fell to the floor in agony but played on as we drew 1-1. Only after I took my boot off and had my foot examined did I realise I had broken a toe on my right foot. That left me with a problem. The doctor said he could inject it to stop the pain, and Brian Little left the decision to me. The only way I could continue to play games was to have the injection so I decided that's what I would do before each game.

Our club doctor injected me before the away game at Cambridge, but for the next few trips we had to rely on the home team's medical staff. An injection shortly before kick off was enough to get me through, until about half an hour or an hour after the final whistle when I couldn't even wear my shoes because of the pain.

This wasn't the ideal scenario, but it enabled me to continue playing, including the return game against Wrighty and co at Highbury when we lost 2-0 and at Watford, where I had another surreal moment before the game.

It was a couple of days before my birthday and again we organised for a GP at the home club to help me out. I was sitting on the treatment table in the physio's room on my own, waiting to be injected, when the door opened, and I couldn't believe it when in walked Watford chairman Elton John. To understand my excitement, you need to know Elton John is my top music idol. I bought all his albums and followed him very closely.

He was confused, pointing out I wasn't one of his team's players. I explained I was a Leicester City player waiting for an arranged injection. I said I was a fan of his and asked to shake his hand. We had a good chat in which I said it was great to meet him but hoped his team wouldn't beat us – we won 1-0. So, I did have something to thank Wrighty for – if he hadn't broken my toe, I would never have met my idol.

The Full Members Cup provided another highlight of my season. We won our way to a two leg semi final against Forest. Apart from the tie at Derby, these were the only times I ever played against my old gaffer's side.

Following a 1-1 draw at Filbert Street, came the moment I was really looking forward to – walking out at the City Ground. Yes, it felt weird not to be in a red shirt, but Forest against Leicester is always a tough local derby and now it was time to do my best for Leicester. Unfortunately, our Wembley hopes were ended by a 2-0 defeat and I got no more than a polite 'how are you son?' from my old gaffer.

My popularity with Leicester fans grew when I became the penalty taker. I developed my own style coming off a one-step run which I practiced a lot in training and became confident I would never miss. This made sense because of the latest rule change. Goalkeepers weren't allowed to move before the ball was struck, so I gave them the least possible time to spring to either side.

I had a good record overall, including slotting one past Shilts against Derby. But my 100 per cent record bit the dust when I missed a penalty to lose a shootout in the FA Cup at Barnsley - I swear the ball ended up in Blackpool – and, worse still, I missed in our last but one game of the season at Charlton when we were still seeking automatic promotion.

We were 2-0 down when the referee pointed to the spot, giving me the chance to put us back in the hunt. I made such poor contact the goalkeeper could have thrown his cap on it. That left us with Kevin Keegan's Newcastle rolling up at Filbert Street on the final day fighting for their Second Division lives. There were fans all around the pitch that afternoon as Walshy helped them out with an own goal as we lost 2-1

That wasn't the perfect preparation for our first crack at the play offs, where we were already expecting a very tough test at Cambridge United after being thrashed 5-1 at the Abbey Stadium earlier in the season. They had a powerful front duo of Steve

Claridge and Dion Dublin, who both became Leicester favourites, not to mention Lee Philpott on the left side. Also, we had to battle a difficult slopy pitch.

We were fairly pleased with a 1-1 draw, but knew the job was far from done going back to Filbert Street. That was one of those special football nights that seem to happen under the floodlights, as we totally battered Cambridge 5-1 to book our date at Wembley.

They now call the play off final the most lucrative game in football, but it's even more important for the players. A 46-game season you start preparing for in the summer ends for two teams in a one-off winner-take-all game that guarantees heartbreak for the losers. I played at Wembley six times in my career and have later been there four times as a manager and I can tell you it's no consolation if you lose.

We were very confident going into the game. We had beaten Blackburn twice, including a recent 1-0 success in their own backyard, and fancied ourselves to get the job done. We called ourselves The Grinders because we believed we could always grind out a result.

There was nothing much between the teams, and the tie was decided in controversial fashion when Walshy put his arm across David Speedie just inside the penalty area and they scored the winning goal from the spot. Was it a penalty? You could argue either way.

Losing to Blackburn was a devastating blow for us. I was one of several players in tears at the end because we had worked so hard for nine or ten months to get into the Premier League and it had all been taken away by a dubious penalty.

It's easy in circumstances like that for teams to suffer a hangover the following season but we handled it well both on and off the pitch. The management didn't panic and make too many changes, and we took the disappointment on the chin and were soon ready to go again.

It's important the right characters are brought into a happy mix and Ian Ormondroyd, Leicester's record signing, and Phil Gee, who like Ian signed from Derby, were just that.

But that was after Ormondroyd scared us all to death on our summer tour of Norway. This is another beautiful country but, rather like Sweden, a place with little to entertain a group of pleasure-seeking footballers. So stuck in a hotel in the middle of nowhere, we were quite enthusiastic when Brian Little invited us all to go clay pigeon shooting. This was something completely new for me and the majority of the lads, so why not? What could possibly go wrong?

The officials at the site gave us a useful talk on the lines of 'always hold your gun to the floor' and 'don't cock your gun until ready to shoot.' We all listened carefully and were split into groups of six. 'Sticks', as we called him because of his slight build, seemed confused from the start, asking further questions about what to do. When it came to his turn, I was sat on a wall behind him with several of the others watching closely. Nothing happened when 'Sticks' pulled the trigger, then he turned around to face us, shouting that it hadn't worked and pointing his gun in our direction! You've never seen a group of footballers disappear so fast.

The man in charge was shouting in Norwegian 'what are you doing?' when 'Sticks', by now pointing his gun to the floor, fired. There was a big bang. How he didn't blow his foot off I'm not sure – but that was one time he was grateful for missing from close range.

Near accidents apart, I was part of a close-knit group of people and looking forward to the new season after being voted player of the year by the fans three times in the previous five years with Leicester and Notts. So, things were going great for me. The man-management of the manager and his team was very good. And whilst never being as quirky and unpredictable as Brian Clough, he did things such as giving us days off from training to meet instead for a coffee and a bite to eat. That sort of thing is very good for morale.

Although he was a lovely bloke and easy to talk to, he was still the boss. Brian Little was one of the managers I learnt from when it was my turn to do the job. He created a family-like atmosphere with everyone included, one reason he had our respect.

I enjoyed and appreciated his attempts to relax us although, through no fault of anyone's, our stay at The Belfry, the world-famous golfing venue, didn't quite go to plan. Three days and two nights away from training playing golf and bonding as a team sounded great. But it all went wrong for me on the eighth hole when I finished up behind a few trees with what looked like a straightforward pitching wedge onto the green.

I took the shot, and the next thing I knew the ball hit me smack in the eye and laid me out. I can still hear the ringing in my head as I recall the story. I remember hearing Walshy, who was in my four ball, calling for help, and an ambulance was rushed onto the course to take me to the eye hospital at Birmingham – so much for my three days away!

I suffered burst blood vessels in the back of my eye and was told to avoid sudden jerky movements over the next couple of weeks, or risk losing sight in my left eye. This was one of those occasions where the club needed to tell a few white lies over why I was out of the team – I think they blamed it on my dodgy hamstring!

It was Brian Little who made me captain for the first time in my career, and again he handled the issue with me and my close mate Steve Walsh very well. Walshy was probably my best friend at Leicester. I still lived near Nottingham and close to the A46, and he was based near Six Hills. So, it made sense for me to park up at a hotel off the A46 and for us to drive into Leicester together, often via McDonald's for a banana milkshake! We did that throughout my five years at the club.

That gave us time to chat about all things Leicester City and to see that, although we were different characters and personalities in some ways, we also had a lot in common. Both of us were winners. Walshy was immense as a player and would never accept defeat, I was brought up with the same attitude through my apprenticeship under Brian Clough and Peter Taylor. The difference was in our discipline. I got it from my childhood, and it was further drilled into me at Forest where we rarely troubled the referees. Walshy sometimes lost it on the pitch and for those few seconds or minutes went out for revenge on whoever he thought had wronged him.

Walshy was Mr Leicester City. Cut him apart, he bled blue and white. And he demanded the same attitude from everyone else at the club. I swear he used half the country's stock of Voltarol just to get him out onto the pitch. Walshy totally got me, and I got him. We all know he had his disciplinary problems when the red mist descended, but we all accepted him as skipper because of who and what he was.

Things, though, came to a head after Walshy had a particularly bad day at Charlton. I'd been chatting with him about toning it down a bit and keeping his temper in check, and he went into print just before the trip to London saying he thought he'd turned the corner.

But that day I turned around and saw him put the nut on Charlton striker Carl Leaburn and the rest was inevitable. The red card came out and we were up against it on the pitch, but more was to follow.

Come the end of the game, everyone was saying 'where's Walshy?'. Our skipper had gone missing. Exactly what happened I don't know, but he eventually got a lift home to Leicester with one of his mates.

The manager had to act the way he did to keep us all together. I'm not saying losing the captaincy wasn't a body blow for him – I know it was. But our relationship meant the unity in the dressing room was preserved. The captain's role is important in football, as the manager expects his skipper to support him and act as a bridge between him and the rest of the team. When Walshy was skipper, I was always there alongside him chipping in my view. Now the roles were reversed, we acted in much the same way.

Instead of being destroyed and discarded, Brian Little cleverly gave Walshy a new role in the side, maybe to take him out of the firing line. Playing the big man up front worked a treat as he bagged a hatful of goals that helped put us on track for another tilt at the play offs. It was also perfect for me and my game.

I usually played on the right side of the back five, with plenty of opportunity to get forward. I had the energy and the desire to get up and down the pitch and it was a role I really enjoyed. Being a good crosser of the ball, I was even happier having a target like Walshy to aim at, and provided a fair few balls for him to nod into the net.

I also loved playing at Filbert Street. The old ground was showing signs of wear and tear, but the atmosphere there was great, particularly as bigger, and bigger crowds started to turn out to support us. Nobody can doubt the impact the new stadium has had on the club's subsequent rise to the top of the English game, but I'm glad I played my football at Filbo.

The fact we had bad runs as well as good ones meant automatic promotion was out of the question, particularly with Kevin Keegan's Newcastle United running riot at the top. But it was still another major achievement to qualify for the play offs even though we could have done without being the guests at the Geordies' promotion party.

It was the last game of the season and nothing on it for either side – Newcastle were champions, and we were safely in the play offs. But, with a big crowd inside St James Park and a carnival-style atmosphere including a live performance from Lindisfarne, they wanted to put on a show, and we were equally determined to be party poopers.

We were six nil down at half time! The scoreline was so shocking a mate of mine said he switched on the TV – the game was broadcast live on Central – and thought the statistic of 6-0 must be the number of corners. The manager did his best to rally us at half time to play for pride and we drew the second half 1-1 with Walshy scoring for us.

Again, it's to our credit we didn't allow such a mauling to affect us when we began our play off campaign against Portsmouth. Filbert Street was already being renovated, so we switched the game to the City Ground, Nottingham, of all places. That went down better with me than it did with most Leicester supporters but, typically, they turned out in big numbers on a very warm Sunday afternoon.

Running down that tunnel meant a lot to me and I had a decent game as we won 1-0 to take a useful, but not decisive, advantage into the second leg. The goal came from Julian Joachim, a young striker just breaking through into the side. The pace, power, and strength he showed to get between two Pompey defenders and stick the ball into the net was breath-taking and gave us something to cling to at Pompey.

That was a huge time in my life with our third child, Ria, being born 24 hours before such an important football match. We went a goal down before Sticks equalised. He was about five yards offside, but never mind! Steve Thompson then increased our overall lead to two goals before the home side equalised on the night and we had to hang on for the final whistle. My joy at an incredible 24 hours in my life was then marred when a young woman spat in my face on the pitch. I still find it shocking that someone actually did that after a football match.

There's always a longish break between the semi final and the final, and we approached the Swindon game positively. Whereas Blackburn had been the bookies' favourites 12 months ago, we were given a slight edge against Glenn Hoddle's side. But what a match that turned out to be.

The first hour or so is hard for me to explain. We expected a close encounter but found ourselves 3-0 down. Ok, Hoddle was a world class player and produced a touch of class for the first goal, but somehow the game had seemingly drifted well beyond us.

The comeback that followed was the most remarkable I ever experienced in a football match and tells you everything you need to know about that Leicester City side. Needless to say, Walshy played a leading part in our comeback, producing a header that was saved for our first goal, then scoring himself. It still sends shivers down my spine when I watch the video and see Steve Thompson firing in our third goal. There we were at 3-3, and suddenly everyone expected us to win.

What happened afterwards was totally heart-breaking. Hoddle played a good ball over the top which had goalkeeper Kevin Poole rushing to the edge of the box to try to get there first. The contact between him and the Swindon player was minimal, if any at all. I was honestly shocked when the referee pointed to the spot. If anything, that was less of a penalty than the one given against Walshy against Blackburn.

We felt like lightning struck twice. There's nothing anyone can say to make you feel better in that situation. The only thing that helps is time. We went through so many raw emotions at Wembley in that one afternoon, let alone all the ups and downs over the whole season.

I learnt another life lesson that night, one I pass on to my players today – beer doesn't taste as good when you've just lost! We booked our 'celebration party' at Sketchley Grange Hotel which turned into the place to drown our sorrows instead. Nevertheless, a few drinks was probably the first stage towards getting our heads back together.

A week in Ibiza gave us another chance to stick together and turn things around. It was a great week, also giving us the chance to have a laugh. One day, a few of us went for a walk including Dave Oldfield, Walshy, Tommy Wright, and Kevin Poole. Now, Pooley is one of the nicest men you will ever meet but also one of the quietest, a tag we put to the test. We decided on a pit stop at a local bar where we sat outside and ordered five beers. Pooley went inside to the toilet just as it started raining. The obvious thing was for us to move inside the bar, but I told the lads to wait for Pooley to come back and see how long it took for him to speak. So, we sat there getting soaked for a full five minutes before Pooley eventually suggested we should move to a huge round of applause from the rest of us.

As Leicester City fans will remember, the following season saw us get rid of our Wembley hoodoo and reach the promised land of the Premier League in highly dramatic circumstances. But it was a bittersweet time for me as niggling hamstring injuries limited me to 22 appearances and prevented me from playing against Derby County in the play off final.

Once again it was an incredible achievement from the lads to put ourselves in the play off frame for a third successive season, before seeing off Tranmere Rovers in the semi final.

Brian Little came up with a very special way of including me on the big day after I'd suffered my latest hamstring pull a couple of weeks earlier. You can only imagine how gutted I was to miss out on the chance of skippering the team as we finally had the chance to achieve our dream after three years of hard work. Yet, the manager found a surprising way of making me feel part of one of the proudest days in the club's history.

What happened is this. I was with the squad at the hotel the night before the game. Because neither David Speedie nor I could play at Wembley we asked the gaffer for permission to have a drink at the bar. Anyway, one drink turned into a few drinks and we sat there laughing and joking until about 4 or 5am. That was a healing process as two experienced pros chatted over events that had been so important in our careers.

Speedo had already made himself a lot more popular with his performances for City that season. As Walshy said in his book, there were no hard feelings – if Speedo had won Leicester a penalty in the same circumstances none of us would have complained. In turn, he was interested in finding out about life playing for Brian Clough, so we shared some stories and laughs about the great man. It was a very special night yet bettered by what was to come.

I felt worried when the gaffer called me over for a chat at breakfast. I honestly thought he was going to have a go at me for being up drinking so late. Instead, he said he'd like me to lead the lads out onto the pitch at Wembley. I was amazed. I didn't fully realise back then how much it meant to a manager to do that. I appreciate that even more today having done the same myself at Gateshead and York.

I felt honoured. I went back to the hotel room and phoned Sue to tell her. I was crying with emotion. Walking onto the pitch felt like I was playing. Even now it makes me think about how much he must have thought of me. It was an incredible gesture. Before the game started, I walked back up to the very top of the stand to take my place with the Radio Leicester commentary team of Neville Foulger and Geoff Peters. That was the first time I was ever asked to do co-commentary, and what a day to do it.

Derby took the lead and had the better of the play until Walshy turned it our way. I knew as much as anyone how close the big man was to not playing. He had been injured and I reckon he must have been on double Voltarol to get himself out on the pitch. He didn't as much as declare himself fit, it was more that he was willing to put his battered body on the line. Walshy scored both goals in our famous 2-1 victory, the winner a few minutes from time is written in club folklore for many reasons.

The Radio Leicester lads won't forget it in a hurry either. I have got a tape of the mayhem in the commentary box when Walshy put the ball into the Derby net. I couldn't contain my excitement. I think I shouted 'Walshy, get in' and grabbed Geoff around the neck whilst he was still trying to get his own words out. That was a sign of my passion for the club. I was back down on the side of the pitch a few minutes later celebrating with the lads after the final whistle.

I couldn't have been happier. Although injuries limited my appearances, I knew I played my part in promotion and was thrilled to be back in the topflight for the first time since leaving Forest. But this time it was in the new-look Premier League.

However, things never went the way I expected. I had come to the end of my contract, with the manager urging me to concentrate on getting the job done – promotion – and then a new deal would be sorted out afterwards. But when I sat down and started talking with Brian Little, it didn't go great. The two-year deal he offered me wasn't anything like what I was hoping for. As I've already said, money was never the big issue for me in my playing career, but it does give you an indication of how you are valued. And, in this case, I couldn't hide my disappointment because the terms were not what I thought I deserved. We kept talking and eventually came to an agreement, but when I signed it wasn't with the same sense of excitement that I had anticipated.

The clues that all was not right kept coming after we returned for pre-season training. One quirk of the Premier League was we had squad numbers with our names on our shirts. I'd worn number two throughout my time at Leicester but was now given squad number 22. The two shirt went instead to Simon Grayson.

Next came a friendly at Port Vale where I was in the team. Coach Allan Evans was in charge and told Walshy to lead the lads out. I had a word with him to ask what was happening. After all, I was the club skipper, but he laughed it off by saying it was only a friendly and I shouldn't take too much notice. Nevertheless, I wasn't feeling comfortable or wanted.

That feeling persisted as I didn't make the side for our opening match back in the big time at home to Newcastle United, nor in the next two fixtures at Blackburn and Forest at the City Ground. Having lost our first three matches, I started my first Premier League game in our 1-1 draw against QPR. I played the 90 minutes at right back and thought I had a decent game, but more disappointment was to come when the gaffer pulled me into his office two days later to say I wasn't going to travel to Wimbledon on the Saturday.

Alarm bells were beginning to ring, so I asked the manager straight. "Gaffer, you've got to be honest with me. Am I not part of your plans?"

He answered quite cautiously, "You are not going to play the games you might like." That told me all I needed to know. He may have been trying to avoid hurting me, but the real answer to my question was 'no'. I was disappointed with the way this was handled, particularly after he had been so good to me at Wembley.

I was 32 years old, very physically fit and knew I still had plenty to offer. Had Brian Little said I wouldn't be a regular starter, but had a part to play in his squad, I'd have accepted it. I could fill in for several positions including either side at full back or in midfield. Yes, he had brought in new players such as Franz Carr and Mark Draper, but I would have been a useful and versatile player to have around.

Other players may well have sulked and stayed around the place picking up their wages. That was never me. My priority was playing football and felt I had no choice but to ask to be put on the transfer list.

That was a sad way for me to go after making 232 appearances for Leicester City from 1989 to 1994. Chatting to The Birch, Alan Birchenall, he thought much the same way. Although Forest gave me great special years and medals, I think my best years as a player were at Leicester because I played consistently. So, the last thing I expected, or wanted, to do was to leave.

CHAPTER 7
I THOUGHT IT WAS ALL OVER!

FIRST to come knocking was Notts County, when new manager Russell Slade rang. Then, chairman Derek Pavis spoke with me: "We want you to come back, my lad!" Everything was agreed, but Mr Pavis, who I always got on well with, said he wouldn't pay big money.

Ok, I thought, I'll see if Leicester, considering the very good service I'd given them over five years, would do me a favour and let me go on a free transfer. Brian Little wasn't sure, but referred the issue to chairman Martin George, and he said City wanted £50,000. I took this back to Mr Pavis and he was very honest. He wasn't prepared to pay Leicester £50k, but had no problem paying that money to me. So, if I persuaded Leicester to let me go for free, I would get a £50k bonus.

Leicester held their ground, however, and Brian Little then told me QPR had also come in. I wasn't interested because I'd agreed to join Notts. Eventually Notts paid the transfer fee and I was off to Meadow Lane. Others may have played hard ball and got themselves a better financial deal out of it; I was more interested in playing regular football.

I shook hands with Brian Little, and the rest of the lads, and was out of Leicester and back at Notts where the Magpies were beginning to struggle in the Second Division. I signed a two-year deal and soon found out it was a very different dressing room from the one I left five years before.

There were plenty of good footballers at Notts – too good to be down at the bottom of the division – but, in my opinion, they lacked discipline and professionalism. I quickly got the impression the squad wasn't together and this was reflected in our disappointing results.

The frustration was that a side who turned in an unbelievable performance in the League Cup to thrash a full-strength Tottenham Hotspur, managed by Ossie Ardiles and with German legend Jurgen Klinsmann in attack, 3-0 in front of nearly 17,000 ecstatic fans at Meadow Lane, couldn't come to terms with far inferior opponents in the league.

It was no surprise when, after a run of five successive defeats, Russell Slade was shown the door and in came Howard Kendall, who had managed Everton to the First Division title and European glory. I liked Howard Kendall, and it was such a pity it never worked out for him at Notts. He was another gaffer who tried hard to relax the players and take the pressure off of us, but without the results to go with it, his methods were open to criticism.

One of the first things he told us was to get a lift into training and take a taxi home. He also booked The Boat Club at the side of the River Trent for lunch and a few drinks. We all had to tell jokes as we tried to build up a good team spirit. That was Howard's way.

I had a lot of respect for Howard because of what he achieved in the game and I got on well with him. He made a positive move bringing in fellow Merseyside star Steve Nicol to bolster our defence and become assistant manager. Steve was somebody I had a lot of respect for and got on well with.

The managerial bounce amounted to two morale-boosting victories before normal service resumed and we hit another bad run. I could see some of Brian Clough in Howard's relaxed ways, but we never looked like we were getting out of trouble.

The only success we enjoyed was in the Anglo Italian Cup. Although this meant little to most Notts fans compared with the drop to Division Three, it was a very positive experience. In the early rounds, I remember being in the square in Milan having a good time and scoring the winning spot kick at the Victoria Ground, as we saw off Stoke City in a shootout to take us to Wembley for the final against Ascoli.

Howard calmed us down by playing his favourite 'chase the ace' card game with us on the coach, but he paid a heavy price for drinking red wine when he spilt some down his shirt with no possible way of hiding an obvious stain. I played left back and was man of the match in a 2-1 victory in my last game at Wembley as a player. I did have an embarrassment, almost as big as Howard's, a kiss on the cheek from big Devon White celebrating his winner. Good job he was such a good mate!

Perhaps there was a clash of personalities between Howard and Derek Pavis as the master manager was on his way just a couple of weeks later. I got an insight into Howard's frustration at Notts shortly before that happened. He left me out of the side and was ready when I knocked on his door. "I know what you are going to say – it's nothing personal, I'm trying something different," he said. "Come and have a beer with me." We spent about three or four hours together and had a couple of beers. He spoke about his time at Everton and I told him about my career at Forest. It was a lovely, lovely occasion. I was pleased Howard felt he could talk with me like that and it increased my respect for him even further.

You are what you are. Everyone manages the way they believe will bring success, and how they are perceived by the fans is not always in line with what they are trying to do. Howard Kendall used the same methods that worked so well at Goodison Park but unfortunately it didn't work out. Notts fans may have thought he was past his best, but I'm not sure that was the case. Because of my experiences across the Trent, I could see what he was doing. I often think back to the afternoon I spent with him and feel privileged to have had that moment with a top man.

Caretakers Steve Nicol and Wayne Jones were the fourth set of people in charge that terrible season, as the previously successful Mick Walker had been relieved of his duties before I arrived. We were in desperate need of stability but, first impressions of our new gaffer in the summer weren't the best.

I have to say the way Colin Murphy introduced, or didn't introduce himself, to the Notts lads, was one of the weirdest things I experienced in football – and, by now, you know I've had more than my fair share.

The players waited in the dressing room for Colin and his assistant Steve Thompson. Colin had been a surprise and brief managerial appointment at Derby and previously worked at Notts, but I knew very little about him. The door opened, Colin walked in and never said a word. Instead, he spent the next few minutes eyeballing all the players in turn before looking at Devon White and saying: "How much did this f---ing club pay for you?"

"£50,000," Devon replied politely.

"Fifty f---ing thousand too much," he added. Then he told us all we were a 'f---ing disgrace for what you have done to this club'. I was taken aback by this. I couldn't see how singling Devon out was justified and he had just made it more difficult to get the rest of us on board as well.

The strange mood continued as Steve Thompson took the training, with Colin remaining silent. Then he gave us a special treat – a pre-season camp at an army barracks that went on for days and days. That was the hardest training I experienced in my life.

We were knocked up at 5am each morning for a five-mile jog, followed by a rigorous swim, and a jog back to the camp for breakfast. Then, we had an incredibly tough session with the army trainers that left us wondering what on earth was going on. Still there was no interaction with the manager who was only succeeding in getting our backs up.

Eventually we got some very hard-earned light relief when Steve Thompson told us there was a pub down the road and the gaffer had given us permission to have a few beers. We enjoyed the drinks and a singsong before going back to the dormitories. After all the physical work, there was no problem going to sleep, but Graeme Hogg, the fomer Manchester United defender, got woken up in a horrible way. Steve Nicol was urinated on him! The whole thing became a farce with Graeme chasing Steve all over the dormitories saying, 'I'm going to kill him'. Poor Steve, half awake and half asleep, had no idea what he was doing.

The torture continued and, after eight or nine days during which the manager hadn't said a word to any of us, we were back home. A rant against Peter Butler, one of the younger players, broke the silence. Again, he was slaughtering us without establishing any real communication.

As the weeks went by, I got on with Colin Murphy better, although I was in and out of his side. Another of his strange ways was coming onto the training pitch with a bag of balls and telling me to kick them against him as hard as I could. I made perfect contact with my first shot but earned a sarcastic remark for 'not being able to hit a barn door' when I missed him. To be fair to the boss, there was some method in his madness. He was trying to get the best out of his players, and he didn't do badly as we reached the Third Division play offs.

My season and career was over long before that however. That came just after Dave Norton, whom I played with during my first spell with Notts, told me Northampton were interested. The prospect of finishing my career, with my home club where Dad was such a hero, excited me, and Murphy was willing to let me go.

But there was no time for the deal to be done because I was injured in a cup tie at York City. Unfortunately, my hamstring nightmare came back to haunt me. I played the ball up the line and felt like I'd been shot in the back of the leg. I was in agony. My hamstring had come away from my bone.

That was the start of the end. I went under the knife to get it put right but couldn't get myself fit again. Eventually I saw a specialist and he recommended I retired from professional football.

That was it. My professional career ended on that sad note. What started with the thrill of playing against Arsenal at a packed City Ground for the First Division champions, ended anonymously on a bleak night at York in a game I can barely remember.

CHAPTER 8
EARLY LESSONS IN MANAGEMENT

By JOHN BARNWELL, former Grantham Town manager

GRANTHAM *officials showed me a list of potential managers when I told them I was leaving and asked my opinion. I told them to add Gary Mills to that list having managed him at Notts County.*

I could not guarantee Gary would be successful, but I knew he would work hard, have the desire to succeed and the quality of being able to learn. Gary justified those words by steering Grantham to promotion in his second season.

I have followed Gary's progress in which he has won promotions and trophies at different clubs. I will say I am very surprised he has not gone on to much bigger and better things in management with a really big club. He needed to be given the right opportunity at the right time because Gary Mills can handle players and the media – both major issues.

*****

By Darron Gee, long term assistant manager to Young Millsy

I'M A FRIEND *as well as a colleague of Gary and, whilst he could have gone a lot further in management, we have had a lot of success and fun along the way.*

He has never had the opportunity to manage a club on the up, even the bigger ones he has worked at were struggling when he took over.

I'd just got Dunkirk promoted when Gary invited me to work with him at Grantham Town. I had more knowledge of Non-

League football and we spent the next few months looking here, there, and everywhere for players.

It was great to get promotion at Grantham and set a record for clean sheets at King's Lynn before we teamed up at Tamworth. I understood Gary's ambition in going to Coventry and was persuaded to stay as the manager at Tamworth where I went on to achieve further success.

Gary told me before we started at Grantham that one day we would get the Notts County job, and he was so thrilled when he rang to say that dream had come true. What happened afterwards was so disappointing. If ever there was a right club at the wrong time, it was Notts. They were in disarray both on and off the field and, although there were lovely people working there, things didn't work out well. I know Gary's heart was 100 per cent in it and he was the man to turn the club around, but he wasn't given the time.

It was sad when, for personal reasons, I couldn't follow him to Gateshead, but there was one thing I didn't miss – the gaffer digging me in the ribs every few minutes.

Gary's an old school manager in the best possible sense. He is a players' manager, he is strict, keeps thing simple, and takes the pressure off the lads who go out onto the pitch.

Of course, he wanted to manage further up, but he's enjoyed all that is great about Non-League football, such as the relationship with the fans, and the brilliant people working behind the scenes to keep smaller clubs in business.

Gary said 'never say never' when I asked him a few years back if we'd ever work together again, and we have since reunited at Corby. We were top of the pile after a few games in 2020 before it all got called off, and we're now looking forward to starting all over again.

Gary's been a great servant to East Midlands football, in particular, over the years, and he should be still in the game. From first meeting in our 20s to today, when we speak almost every day, I can't remember one major argument. But, yes, he still digs me in the ribs!

*****

THE hamstring injury that finally forced me to retire from professional football happened first in America.

Late in the play off semi final I felt a twinge in the back of my leg. I was lucky the Soccer Bowl final was a few weeks later and I was fit to play.

From then on, I was always aware of my hamstring which eventually caused me to miss Leicester's big play off final against Derby. The constant strain over the years probably led to my final injury. I've never experienced pain like I did at York. It's a nightmare injury that takes about six weeks to recover from. To make it worse, you feel you can come back quicker than you can.

An MRI scan showed the muscle had come away from the bone completely. I needed surgery including drilling a hole into the bone to reattach the hamstring. I made it back into training, but it wasn't the same. I felt restricted. I went to see a specialist and he recommended I retire. Notts agreed with my decision and were kind enough to offer me a benefit match that took place later that year.

I felt gutted for many reasons, not least that I lost the chance to finish my career at Northampton. The Cobblers were watching me at York that night and Notts manager Colin Murphy had been honest with me and backed the move.

Other than the hamstring, I was as fit as a fiddle and knew I had a couple more years in me at least. So that made retiring even tougher. You know as a footballer you can't go on forever, but I never felt the end was near until that last injury.

Going into management was what I wanted to do. Having been skipper at both Leicester and Notts, I knew how I wanted my players to train, play, and conduct themselves, mostly based on how I was as a player. Even in training I wanted to win. When playing eight versus eight, I wanted to be on the winning side. And I had the discipline from my upbringing and the best possible apprenticeship at Forest. For me, discipline and a love for the game are musts for a manager, and I was well qualified.

As always, Sue was my rock when I needed it most. We were both aware how difficult footballers can find life after their playing days are over, but she went to great lengths to reassure me from day one things would be ok. She was great with me at that important time.

As it turned out, my phone went just a couple of weeks later, and then things started to happen. John Barnwell, my former

Notts boss, said he was sorry to hear I had been forced to retire and knew I wanted to go into management. He invited me to lunch at a pub in Gunthorpe to discuss an idea.

I was so grateful to John for thinking of me. We had never directly discussed my managerial aims when I played for him, but with us both being football men he picked it up.

John explained he was manager of Grantham Town but was leaving to become Chief Executive of the newly formed League Managers' Association. He had already told the Grantham chairman I was the man to appoint!

Although we got on so well, I knew John wouldn't have done this had he not genuinely thought I would make a good manager.

I told him I was definitely interested and he said the chairman Alan Prince would be in touch. I've got to admit that at this stage I knew very little about Non-League football having gone straight from youth football into the professional game. A quick piece of research revealed they were in the Southern League Midland Division and being watched by about 150 fans. This was a whole new world for me, having never managed before nor had contact with the game at grass roots level.

My ambition was to manage at the same highest level I had played at. But, like Brian Clough whose first job was at Hartlepools, I was more than happy to begin further down. I had to start somewhere, so why not Grantham Town?

My only previous experience of the club came when I bumped into Martin O'Neill in a restaurant off the A52 a couple of years earlier. He was managing The Gingerbreads and invited me to a charity evening hosted by the former Manchester United manager Tommy Docherty.

I met Alan Prince and had a 20-minute interview, which felt like I had already got the job before we started talking. It was pre-season when I joined and there was no time to lose. My first move was to find someone who knew more about this level of football to work as my assistant.

The man was Darron Gee. I knew him as a former footballer who had lived with my sister-in-law Karen, and was manager of Dunkirk, a Nottinghamshire-based side. His initial response was positive, but he was happy at Dunkirk, so I had to persuade him. We had a friendly with Anstey Nomads, so I invited him to have a look.

I said we would go on to higher things, and the first professional club we would manage together would be Notts County.

That nearly went out of the window after 20 minutes of the game, when Darron turned round to me and said: "This lot are shite, I've got better players at Dunkirk." I knew he had the knowledge and contacts to help build a better team and, fortunately, I managed to convince him to come.

I had one surprise for him at our first training session on the Saturday. I wanted us to look smart, professional, and on the same page, so I went into a sports shop in Nottingham and bought us some training kits. The best I could get was black and green Norwich City gear which fitted the bill for the look I was after.

The other surprise was that Grantham's ground was being used by the famous Dutch side Ajax, so we had to slum it nearby. But that was nothing compared with the culture shock of when we kicked off our league season away at Redditch United.

Non-League grounds were new to me and this wasn't one of the best. I paced up and down the pitch from goalmouth to goalmouth- something I started that day and have continued ever since – and it looked like the penalty spot was too close to the edge of the box. I soon found out why – the 18-yard box was only 15! That was when I wondered what on earth I had got myself into.

The ref gave us the option of postponing the game. Welcome to Non- League football, Gary. I decided there was no point going home without a game, so we went ahead.

That game was also my first as a player after officially retiring. My hamstring was a lot better, if not properly right, and I was keen to carry on playing if possible. My overall fitness was good, so I began my managerial career at right back. It wasn't the greatest of starts though. We lost 1-0 and I discovered how it feels to be a manager. Losing as a player is bad enough, losing as a manager seemed like the end of the world.

To make things worse, I went into the clubhouse and the chairman never said a word. I saw him with a director and the club's secretary, and he gave me the silent treatment. That evening I told Sue I needed to tackle this head on. So, I phoned Mr Prince and said I wanted to meet next day. He was surprised but agreed. I told him I'd been in charge for one game, we had lost 1-0 and he didn't speak with me, was that the way it was going to be? I was disappointed to have lost but asked him never to ignore me again. This was a very steep learning curve, and I didn't want to start on the wrong footing.

Things didn't get much better in game two – my home debut. In the Leicester United side that night was my Foxes chum Ali Mauchlan, and he did me no favours. The score was 2-2 when Ali unleashed a shot from 25 yards to win it for the visitors in the last minute. "Thanks very much," I said as we walked off together – or something like that!

Two defeats out of two was a very bad start, but we then had a stroke of luck. Unbelievably, Leicester United folded as a club the very next day – perhaps Ali had asked for a rise! That meant our defeat was struck from the records and we kicked off on the Saturday with only one loss to our name. If only Redditch had folded as well, eh?

All this meant facing Evesham felt like a fresh start, and we took full advantage. We won 3-2 and I scored my first goal for Grantham. It felt just the same as scoring against Manchester United, Arsenal, and Leeds, as I did at Forest. I set off for the corner flag to celebrate and felt a bit of a Charlie when nobody else came to greet me – perhaps it was because I was the boss.

We began to find our feet after that win and, with Darron's big help, I started to feel at home. Darron had a few players for me to watch from local Sunday football. We went to various parts of Nottingham to see lads he thought might be able to step up to a higher level. That was how I made Andy Frawley my first ever signing as a manager. When I invited him to a pub for a chat, I had my mathematics worked out in my head – a playing budget of £500 a week, with one of my players on £100, didn't leave much for the rest of the squad.

I worked out I could offer Andy £25 and he asked for £30, with one condition attached - a new pair of boots! This was new to me, so I rang 'Geebo' (that's Darron). He told me to say 'yes' and that he had spare boots in his loft. Done deal. So, I signed Andy Frawley and got used to dealing with different figures than in the professional game.

Andy made a very impressive debut in a 3-1 win at Raunds Town. The home goalkeeper was shouting 'they're taking the piss' as my new signings Andy Frawley, Ashley Brandy, Neil Glasser, and 'Norm' Parkes played keep ball. This was how I wanted to play, with good possession, rather than banging it long and chasing.

I look back now on some of those early signings with a lot of pleasure. There were lads playing Sunday football or for local sides who didn't know how good they were or could be. I asked what level they thought they could play at and we worked together to make that happen. It was all about helping them become the best footballers they could be. If they bought into that, fine; if not, I was honest with them and they moved on.

One player I had to bide my time to sign was Dave King, a striker banging in goals for Shepshed Dynamo. This taught me another harsh lesson about my new status. I got hold of his phone number and made him an offer to sign for Grantham. Then I got a phone call in the clubhouse. The Shepshed manager was all f------ this and f------ that, saying I hadn't followed the rules. What rules? I hadn't a clue what he was talking about.

Unlike in professional football, I needed to give seven days' notice of an approach for a non-contract player. That was the first I had heard of it, so I said sorry and moved on. We signed Dave King later in the season.

One signing that didn't quite come off was my own brother Graham. He was playing for Harpole and I thought he was more than capable of giving it a go but, after a couple of games, it became clear the travelling was too much for him.

I was enjoying the joint role of playing and managing and, with my fitness levels improving, the thought went through my head; I had retired from professional football too soon. Never mind, I was happy, the players were happy, and the club was happy, with more fans coming through the gates. After averaging 200 the previous season, crowds went up to nearly 300, with even bigger turnouts for FA Trophy games.

The Trophy is Non-League's version of the FA Cup and is beginning to be treated the same way. National League clubs today in particular chop and change their teams and prioritise the league, but I always regarded it as a major competition. I got my first taste of it as we saw off Leek Town, a team on their way to the Conference, then Winsford United.

We defeated Buxton in a replay after I missed a spot kick in the original 1-1 draw, before an epic marathon tie against Blyth Spartans. The thought of one replay, let alone two, would traumatise clubs these days but we were more than grateful for a third chance.

The first game allowed us to build up our team spirit as we got permission to have an overnight stay. Mum and Dad joined me on the team bus, and there was another Harpole connection, with our goalkeeper Peter Bulliman coming from the village.

Blyth were in a higher league and had John 'budgie' Burridge, the former Villa keeper, between the sticks. He didn't look like getting beaten as we trailed 1-0 going into the 90th minute. It was only me and Andy Bullimore at the back as we threw everyone else forward to try to get an equaliser. With 30 seconds left, Darren Grocock got the goal, and I've got a vivid image of Grantham secretary Pat Nixon jumping for joy.

In the dressing room, I learnt another lesson. At first, I was annoyed when director George Freestone walked through the door as I was talking to the lads. George was Grantham mad and came to the games with wife Marj, and what he did that day has stuck with me forever. After I half told him off, he said he had come to congratulate us and had got everyone a £5 bonus. It was from his own pocket – and he wasn't a rich man – and, he had even gone to the bother of changing the notes, so he could hand us all a fiver.

That made my team talk easy. I couldn't thank George enough – not primarily for the money, but for his spirit. He and Pat showed what it meant to follow a football club and that's what I passed onto the players. Our Trophy run ended in the next round, but it helped to reconnect the town with the club that season.

Another overnight stay when we drew Canvey Island in the FA Cup helped me connect with the players. I knew Andy Bullimore, who had a very good centre back partnership with the experienced Adrian Speed, liked a fag and a pint. That was no problem because of the job he was doing on the field.

I told the players to prepare for the game on the Friday night the same way they would back home. Players who usually went to bed early should do so, if they wish, those who liked a drink and went to bed late should be themselves.

I was building trust. Give them some rope, believing they'd be fully focused come 3pm on Saturday. Also, they needed to trust me.

I went out for a walk with Darron and called into a pub for a pint of Guinness before going back to our hotel at about 10.30pm. I spotted Andy at the bar dipping down to avoid me seeing him. I told Andy to come out of hiding and asked him how many drinks he had had. "Three," he said.

"How many do you usually have on a Friday?" I asked.

"Five or six," he replied.

"Stay and have another two or three – I will buy you one," I said. That helped him trust me, and I knew what my centre back was all about. He enjoyed himself on a Friday night, but was always in good nick on Saturday. I was getting the best out of him and he was getting the best out of me.

The first lessons I learnt in management were to be myself, use methods I had seen work for managers, and avoid those that didn't.

People often ask whether I model my management on Brian Clough. The answer is yes and no. I would be a fool not to take note of what he did as a manager. I take his message of simplicity. Football isn't a complicated game. But, with that simplicity came great discipline, and that has always been very important to me.

I would be arrogant to do things 100 per cent my way and not take ideas from what I experienced as a player. Even aside from Brian Clough, I played for some top managers and, if you don't learn from them, you don't deserve to be working in the game.

It's all about trying to get the best out of myself and everyone else. I realised it's tough at non-league level because the players generally aren't full time professionals. But that doesn't mean they can't be professional. Some players are willing to listen, others aren't. They're the ones I sit down with, wish them all the best, but say they aren't for me.

Aided by great performances, including a 4-0 win at Sutton Coldfield when Andy 'six pints' Bullimore produced two wonder strikes, and a Dave King and Dave Taylor-inspired five goal demolition of Corby, we took our promotion challenge to the final game before missing out by two points.

Naturally, I was disappointed. Going up would have been the perfect start for me as a manager, but I was pleased with the progress we made. I was happy at Grantham but, if circumstances had been different, I may have left that summer after an out-of-the-blue call from my good friend Derek Pavis at Notts.

Sam Allardyce was manager of the Magpies and Derek Pavis wanted me as his assistant. I said I was settled at Grantham but interested enough to go down to Meadow Lane for a chat with the future England manager. I had never met Sam, but we spent a couple of hours talking about how he liked to do things and what I was all about. I got the impression it was the chairman's idea I worked alongside the manager, rather than Sam's. In the end the deal failed to materialise. I was grateful that Derek Pavis thought of me, but I was more than content to continue my job with the Gingerbreads.

New summer signings, including former Forest mate Steve Sutton in goal, and former Leicester midfielder Paul Ramsay, helped me get a good side ready for the 1997/98 season, when my team took off. We won our first 11 games of the season, and later put together a run of 12 more.

The most remarkable game of the season – and possibly of my career – was against Corby Town. We were top of the league, they were bottom. When we were 5-1 up, we looked likely to get eight or nine, but somehow, they clawed their way to 5-5 before we got a late winner.

A sign of our progress was that we attracted our biggest league crowd at The South Kesteven Stadium for the visit of local rivals Ilkeston, and we won 6-0. We also went on another good run in the FA Trophy. Penalties proved our strong point, as Steve Sutton saved a spot kick to earn us a replay against Leigh, where we eventually triumphed in a shootout.

We also had brilliant away support, as we overturned a 2-0 deficit to win 3-2 at Bath City, and more than 2,000 fans saw us knock out Conference leaders Hednesford 2-1. About 3,600 turned out for the quarter final against Southport, before 250 and 300 fans went to Liverpool where we lost the midweek replay. We were playing attacking football and entertaining our fans. I don't think Grantham had seen anything like it before.

There was another secret to our success and team spirit. We played a lot of away games in the Birmingham area, and enjoyed dropping into The Anchor Inn in Kegworth just off the A42 on the way home. I had an affinity with it as the landlord, Barry, came from Harpole. The lads used to shout 'Anchor' as soon as we got off the A42. When either Steve Sutton or I were caught talking about our Forest days, the players started singing the famous Mary Hopkins tune *Those were the Days* to bring us back to the present day.

We clinched promotion with seven games left, but I wanted to go up in style by winning the league. I was looking forward to good news when the chairman invited me to talk about a new contract. That meeting changed everything. He said how happy he was and there was a three-year deal waiting for me. Then came the conditions – he wanted me to get rid of all the players and my assistant manager because he was bringing in Danny Bergara to work alongside me. Talk about bursting my bubble, I couldn't believe what I was hearing. Apparently new backer Reg Brealey, the former Sheffield United chairman, was putting money in and the club was planning to go full time.

There were several reasons I couldn't be part of it. I had built a bond with the players who were doing brilliantly for Grantham, and I'd already started to talk about my plans for the following season. By telling them and Darron they were no longer wanted, I'd be letting a lot of people down. That's not me. All this to work with a guy I had never met, and for a project I didn't believe in.

I shocked the chairman by tearing his contract into tiny pieces in front of his eyes. I couldn't begin to tell you the pain I felt. I knew my team could have won the Southern Premier League the following season and I was very happy at Grantham. Now that was all gone.

This was a new lesson for me in management, and I didn't know how to handle it. How was I going to deal with the last few games of the season, and winning the title, when I knew what was around the corner for me and for them?

I told John Barnwell the full story. He was taken aback but gave me very interesting advice. He was against me resigning there and then. He suggested contacting a journalist from the local paper, talking to him in confidence, and at least partly putting him in the picture. Then he would be better informed when the bombshell came at the end of the season.

I told Darron I was going to see the season through for the fans and the players and then resign. We went into our last game at home to Stourbridge needing a point to ward off Ilkeston's challenge and clinch the league. That we did with a 1-1 draw and I allowed the lads to celebrate before telling them the bad news.

Now I needed to explain the truth to the supporters. I went to a fans' meeting and told them the full reasons for my resignation. I said I didn't want to go but didn't fit in with the club's new plans and that's why I had put myself out of work. I said we had got something special at Grantham, but that had all been taken away by the chairman. Nobody in their right mind would have accepted that contract offer. It was a matter of principle.

During two seasons at Grantham, I played 96 games and very much enjoyed my first experience as a manager. But, if I thought my phone was going to ring quickly with a new job offer, I was sadly mistaken. I applied, unsuccessfully, for a few jobs in management, and applied for a driving job with a company in Northamptonshire. It was there I had a surreal experience when, as I was having the interview, there was a knock on the door and Dad walked in. The guy interviewing me was surprised, particularly as Dad worked for a rival company! Dad explained who he was and that he had dropped in to see if I was alright. Good job I love you, Dad!

I was still out of work come the presentation night in Bournemouth, and I was due to receive my Southern League manager of the year award. I was very grateful for the company of an old friend. Gaz Birtles had taken over as Gresley Rovers manager from Paul Futcher and invited me to sit at his club's table.

We were a few tables away from the Grantham party, so it was a little awkward. I booked a hotel with Sue, and our friends Polly and Pam, and generally had a great night. I passed close to the Grantham lads on my way to and back from picking up the award, and had a good time chatting to Gaz and the Gresley lads. Gaz knew I wanted to get back into management but invited me to play for Gresley until I was fixed up.

I played a couple of friendlies and seven league games for Gresley, I enjoyed being with them before the King's Lynn job became available. I submitted my CV and got an interview at the Southern Premier League club where my former Leicester teammate Tony Spearing was in temporary charge.

I was pleased to get the job and felt the potential was massive. They were very well supported by around 1,000 home fans in a nice stadium. At one stage we were unbeaten on our own pitch for a year.

Norfolk isn't the easiest place to attract players to, but Darron helped me build the squad. We sometimes held training night in a different location to help accommodate players with further to travel.

The budget was quite good, and we got plaudits for the football we played, as we finished tenth and fifth in my two seasons in charge.

I combined managing King's Lynn with running a part time printing business, Normil, with Dave Norton, whom I played with at Notts County. We also sold sports equipment combined with after school coaching. Normil was more Dave's thing than mine, although we worked out of my double garage at home.

I took pleasure from our last game of the millennium – a 2-0 at Boston United. We were looking to maintain a promotion tilt in the New Year, with Lee Wilson banging in the goals. Whilst I was in Scotland seeing in the new century, we organised a friendly against Arnold Town to keep the lads ticking over, and Lee Wilson broke his leg in an accidental collision with Bryn Gunn of all people. When Darron phoned to tell me the news, I knew we would be up against it as Wils was our main striker.

The following season started well and my departure in November 2000 wasn't planned. Again, a harsh lesson about management led me to put myself out of a job.

I was called into the boardroom and told the budget was going to be cut. This meant getting rid of several players and Darron. It almost felt like déjà vu after my disappointment at Grantham. To make things worse, the club took my sponsored car off me and suggested I catch the train to get to training and to games.

I knew it was me who really needed to go and the reason that wasn't happening – I was on a contract and they didn't want to pay compensation. Instead, they were pushing me nearer and nearer the exit door, hoping I would resign.

I wasn't happy to carry on, so phoned vice chairman Colin Nicholls to explain. I felt we couldn't be competitive, and I wasn't able to do the job. I wanted a settlement from the club and he offered £1,000, asking me to come to the ground in a couple of hours to collect the cheque. I agreed but heard words that spoke volumes. He didn't put the phone down, and I heard him say 'get in' to his wife and explain that I'd resigned and that it was a great deal for the club. I wasn't that bothered, but it's sad when you find out what people are really like.

I wished him and the club all the best when I collected the cheque and said my goodbyes, offering some advice – when ending a phone call, always make sure you put the receiver down!

Altogether I played 80 games for King's Lynn, mostly in midfield, and was still very competitive at nearly 40 years old. Also on the management side, I knew I had done well – but once again I was out of work, not knowing where my next job was coming from.

CHAPTER 9
MY DREAM JOB BECOMES A NIGHTMARE

By STEVE WALSH, former Tamworth defender.

After playing with Gary at Leicester, I found him to be a great manager when I went to play for him at Tamworth at the end of my career.

There was a touch of Cloughie about him, and perhaps a little of Martin O'Neill too. He was one of the lads, and we all wanted to win for him because we liked him. I enjoyed coming out of retirement to help him, and the club had success.

Looking at his managerial career, it would have been great if Gary had got a chance at a bigger club, but these things happen in football.

*****

MY FIRST two jobs as a manager taught me a great deal – lessons that helped make me the man and the football manager I am today.

Yes, they opened my eyes to how ruthless this game can be, and that was highlighted even more by what happened in the next few years. I felt I had done well at both Grantham and King's Lynn before both chairmen made it impossible for me to stay. I'm not making excuses - merely stating facts.

Managing in non-league football isn't the same as being with a glamour club. I found out it wasn't just a case of putting on my manager's jacket and running the team. A manager at that level gets involved in almost every aspect of the club – and I enjoyed it.

Money was a factor in both exits. The money they wanted to pump into Grantham, which never took them to the heights they expected, and the money that ran out at King's Lynn when we were getting known for playing good football.

I had the printing business with Dave to fall back on, but, as far as football was concerned, I had no idea what was coming next. I was out of the game for about two weeks when I got the chance to play for Conference side Boston United. How that came about I can't really remember. But it was never going to work out because the manager's principles and disciplines were the complete opposite to mine.

But when the Tamworth managerial job became available, I applied straightaway and got myself an interview. I hit it off with Tamworth chairman Bob Andrews immediately. It wasn't difficult for him to sell the club to me because I had fond memories playing there in the FA Trophy. I remembered it was a passionate club, certainly not an easy place for a visiting side to play at, with a good feeling about the place.

I told Bob I was happy to work without a contract until the end of the season – that way he could find out what type of guy I was and the club could get used to me. I was keen to carry on playing and Tamworth gave me that opportunity. I was also pleased to get Geebo back to help with the assistant manager's role, even if we occasionally disagreed when he held up my number to substitute me.

I knew The Lamb was a great place to work and I wanted to be a player's manager. I put trust in those players to play and express themselves, and looked for lads who had ability, and were the right characters both on and off the pitch.

One of the joys of non-league football is the staff and volunteers. Aside from the chairman, I made a couple of life-long friends at Tamworth – kit man Buster Belford and Degsy Bond who worked alongside him. Full time clubs take such things for granted but having someone like Buster who took it on himself to wash the kit is a big thing at that level.

Altogether, the people at Tamworth were brilliant. General manager Russ Moore was another who did a great job – nothing was too much trouble, and everything was done professionally and well. This was one reason why going to Tamworth seemed like a step up for me.

My mission in that first season was to keep Tamworth out of relegation trouble. It went well from the start when I scored in my first game – a draw against Havant and Waterlooville – and we achieved our aim comfortably, finishing 12th. A few clubs were beginning to sniff around me, particularly as I wasn't on a contract, but I was pleased to sit down with chairman Bob at the end of the season and agree a two-year deal. I'd very quickly fallen in love with the place.

The fans were just as I remembered from my days as an opponent, and I felt a good sense of camaraderie with them. I made changes, brought players in, kept the better ones, and things went very well for us in the 2001/2 season.

Team spirit was developed on and off the field. I took the players tenpin bowling and for a pint. It's amazing what you find out about people in a social setting. It wasn't about getting legless but being sensible. It helped them find out about my personality and me discover more about them.

You must be mindful these are not full-time professionals. Players in non-league football usually have jobs and you only see them for a couple of hours training on a Tuesday and Thursday – four hours a week. I wanted them to enjoy themselves during those times. There was no point in making things difficult or boring. To get the best out of them, they needed to be happy to come to training.

One of the lessons from my Forest days I took into my own managerial career was not to talk much about our opponents. To be honest, we never knew that much about them anyway! Instead, the talk was all about us. Why tell my full back how good their right winger is and that he can do this and that? I concentrated on how good our players were and what they were capable of.

It's one of my best achievements as a manager, in my view, that many players have said they enjoyed playing for me. A happy environment is often a successful one.

Our promotion bid went down to the final game. We needed to win at Folkestone to clinch it, whilst Kettering could pip us if they won and we dropped points. That proved to be a memorable, gutting afternoon.

Injury ensured I was confined to my managerial role where I ensured I kept in touch with events elsewhere. I couldn't really avoid the Kettering score anyway as fans were virtually on top of me and told me they were winning. Alongside me on the bench was Steve Walsh, my best mate from Leicester City. I had signed him during the season, but he was also injured and the best we could do was name him as substitute.

We were 3-1 down when I turned to Walshy and said: 'you're going to have to go on'. As so often, he made a difference, scoring one of the goals as we dragged the score back to 3-3 with a few minutes to go. But try as we might, we couldn't get the winner, so missed out on going up.

That was a big disappointment – like the dramatic play off defeats we suffered at Leicester. But what can you do? I dusted myself down, went on holiday, and started making my provisional plans for the following season.

Then came a bolt from the blue – the Sky Blues to be exact. Gary McAllister, whom I played with at Leicester and got on well with, had been given his first managerial role with Eric Black as his assistant. He wanted me at Coventry City as a coach. This was something new and not what I bargained for. I was a manager rather than a coach, but the prospect of joining a Championship club appealed.

It wasn't an easy decision to leave Tamworth. Not at all. That was a massive and tough call to make because I was very happy at The Lamb. Bob Andrews was gutted when I told him but understood my position. We had a good relationship, good enough for me to recommend Geebo who got given the job to build on what we had started. And I'm glad to say that's exactly what happened.

Coventry weren't in the best of shapes. It was a few seasons since their long tenure in the Premier League had come to an end, and they were struggling in the Championship. But it's the sort of challenge you get used to. Most new appointments come because things aren't going well, it's up to you to go in and make a difference.

My role was adapted a little as Gary was still playing. That meant Eric Black and I were usually on the bench for first team matches. I helped Eric take training sessions although he was the main man, and I learnt a lot from him. I also took charge of our reserve team.

Another golden character who started on the same day was Alan Hodgkinson. He introduced himself as the club's new goalkeeping coach and we got on famously from the word go. Hodgy was a former England goalkeeper, who won five full caps between 1957 and 1960, and a Sheffield United legend, having kept goal at Bramall Lane from 1954 to 1971. He was a terrific guy who took great pride in all he did – God rest his soul, he passed away a few years back.

I will always remember Hodgy saying 'make sure when they put that lid on, you have a massive smile on your face'. At his funeral, I looked at his coffin and imagined he was laying there with that smile. What a man!

Going to Coventry was an eye opener, not least because of how much the professional game had changed in the few years since I retired at Notts. The introduction of the Bosman rule had increased player power and silly money started to flood the game for the first time.

I don't want to go into details, but I couldn't believe the money some of the Coventry lads were earning. Most of this was going to players who, in my opinion, weren't good enough to cut it in the Championship. I was 41 years old and told Eric and Gary I reckoned I could have done a better job than some of them.

On the managerial side, too, I had to accept I was stepping back. Gary and Eric were good listeners and happy to ask for my view, but the buck stopped with them.

Strikers Lee Hughes and Julian Joachin, the former Leicester player, were two of the better known names in the Coventry squad, alongside a high number of foreign players. I was there for about 18 months, during which the team continued to struggle without falling through the trap door to League One.

I have a lot of respect for Gary McAllister. He was a high-quality player, who has more recently played for Liverpool. His methods weren't always what I was used to. I'd never taken part in Sunday morning training, even after a beating the day before, nor sat through videos of how the team lost late at night after a long away trip.

Gary was, and is, a perfectionist, and I can't fault him for that. He knew the way he wanted Coventry to play but, unfortunately, I don't think the players were good enough to do it.

He had a difficult time at Cov for several reasons, not least his personal problems. His wife was extremely ill with cancer, and that eventually led to him stepping down. I can only say how sorry I was when I heard that she had passed away, but I'm delighted he is doing so well now as Steven Gerrard's assistant at Rangers.

There were a few surprises for me at Highfield Road, not least at Christmas. Gary said there was a man coming with some Christmas gifts and invited me and Hodgy into his office. I was expecting selection boxes but instead he had Rolex watches costing £10k plus. Hodgy and I soon left the room!

That was nothing compared with our pre-season tour of Germany. We were there for about 10 days based in a lovely hotel with physios doing massages, afternoon naps, and a generally much more scientific approach. All this was a bit of a culture shock for me, but how the game has changed.

First, I've got a confession to make to Andy, our kit man. You need to know that Andy was a great bloke and a biggish chap who liked his food. Now imagine that juicy steak you never want to end - there's always that last piece you save before having to admit defeat.

That was the scenario with Andy, as Gary played a prank on him. He distracted Andy from his food just long enough for me to sweep in with my fork and nick his last piece of steak. Andy was furious. "Who has had my steak?" he roared. One by one we denied it and he never found out the culprit – until now, maybe!

More serious was how a relaxing trip down the river turned into a real problem. Everything was quiet and nice, but the boys were getting bored. So, I suggested to Gary that we let the lads have a drink at the bar and we joined in too. One drink led to another and soon we were having fun with one or two of us, including me, taking turns to be pushed overboard.

Later we had dinner together and a few more drinks at a bar which had a band on. All was going well – as far as I knew. Eric and I went back to the hotel and, after Eric went to bed, I stayed down with one of the players for a last drink. Suddenly I had a tap on my shoulder from a stranger trying to attract my attention.

His English wasn't the best, but he asked if I was in charge of the Coventry group. I tried to explain I was and I wasn't when he said: "Your players are in jail!" I thought he was having a laugh. They were perfectly alright the last time I saw them, but he insisted there had been trouble.

It was already midnight and he was talking about driving me to this jail 40 minutes away to sort things out. Gary and Eric were both in bed and I didn't want to wake them up. So, I had no choice. The journey was lengthy and the last bit along a rickety road went on for ever. Add the fact that I was tired after a few drinks, and in a car with a person I didn't know from Adam.

Eventually, we got there. We were at police cells rather than a prison. The man spoke to the officer in charge and translated his words for me. There were ten in the cells and here was a list of the names – did I recognise them? I knew only two, so realised the others must have given false names.

The officer was willing to release them. The incident had been something or nothing, a scuffle at worst, but he needed their passports before letting them go. Passports? Shit, they were back in the hotel!

Again, I had no choice. So, the man took me another 40 minutes back on the rickety road, and back to home base. I knew which rooms the lads were in, but this was no simple task. I collected the keys for each room, then had to search them one by one for the passports. That took an hour, but I managed to do it.

The German must have been a saint. He waited patiently all that time and was prepared to take me back to the cells. So, another 40 minutes down the rickety road and I thought we were going to crack it. The guy in charge studied the passports, nodded, then said: "2,000 Euros." What? He hadn't said anything about money. But he wouldn't back down and, of course, I didn't have that kind of money on me.

So, we had another 40 minutes along the rickety road whilst I plucked up the courage to wake up Gary and Eric. It was about 3.30am, not the best time to knock on the boss' door. Knock, knock. "Fuck off, Millsy!"

"Let me in!"

He probably thought I'd been drinking all night and carried on. It was a close call whether 'fuck off, Millsy' or 'let me in' would win the day. Finally, Gary let me in. He wasn't in the best of moods and telling him 10 players were in jail didn't go down well.

I was named Player of the Year in my first season at Notts County.

Scoring for Notts from 20 yards with my left foot in a local derby against Mansfield at Meadow Lane in 1988.

John Barnwell put together a very talented team at Notts, but we narrowly missed out on promotion. I'm second from right on the front row.

In action for Leicester against Newcastle in 1991.

Scoring a penalty against Barnsley in 1992.

Celebrating my first Leicester City Player of the
Year award with Sue.

Leicester City player of the year for a second time with Brian
Little and Tommy Wright.

Meeting Prince Charles at Filbert Street – made possible by Barrie Pierpoint, the flamboyant chief executive of Leicester City.

Showing off my flexibility before a game for Leicester.

I became club captain in 1993 which was a huge honour.

Leading out Leicester for the 1993 play off final against Glenn Hoddle's Swindon Town at Wembley.

**Lining up as captain in front of 35,000 City
fans gave me goosebumps.**

Trying to take the ball from Glenn Hoddle.

We won the Anglo-Italian Cup in my
second spell at Notts County.

I am proud to have a full trophy cabinet from football
but one medal is still missing

Double celebration with all my family: my 21st birthday and engagement party that went on long into the night!

How young do we look? My happiest day when I married Sue at Ruddington Church in 1983.

**With my beautiful wife Sue and beautiful children
Ryan, Jenna and Ria.**

Relaxing in Portugal with Sue and the children.

**Beating my good friend Polly at cribb yet again!
Polly drove Mum and Dad the length and breadth
of the country to follow me as a player and manager
and I will always be very grateful.**

Sue has been my rock throughout the years.

I began my managerial journey at Grantham Town.

Winning the Conference North with Tamworth in 2009.

Keeping fit in my 40s at Tamworth with my assistant Geebo. I played my final professional game there aged 48.

Darron Gee and I won FA Trophy and Conference play off final with York City in 2012.

What a feeling!

**The York City supporters are magnificant
and they turned out in force to celebrate with us.**

Celebrating with the York City players.

**Visiting the Angel of the North en route
to Wembley with Gateshead in 2014.**

**Darren Caskey and I took Gateshead to the
Conference play off final in 2014.**

**Leading out Gateshead for their first trip to
Wembley was a proud moment.**

Family celebrating York City's second FA Trophy victory in 2017. With Mum, Martyn, Angela and Graham - and I couldn't leave my wonderful Dad out!

Celebrating VE Day with Sue, Jenna, Ryan and Ria during lockdown.

The unlikely story had to be explained until Gary got the message I was telling the truth. Then Gary joined me and the man in the car going down the rickety road with 2,000 Euros to rescue the lads.

When we got there, the price had gone up to 3,000! We couldn't believe it; this was getting more and more crazy. Gary contacted the organiser of the trip to get him down to the police station to sort everything out. Finally, the players were released and we arranged taxis to drive them back along the rickety road to the hotel. It was about 7am by the time the whole crazy episode was over. Little did I know when I suggested the players had a drink it was going to cause such mayhem.

My time at Coventry was nearly cut short a couple of months later when Telford United were interested in taking me on as manager. I spoke with Gary, and he wasn't keen on me going, but I explained that I still regarded myself more as a manager than a coach. As it happened, the move never materialised, but then came the one I'd been waiting for.

I'd always envisaged working at Notts County, as I told Darron when we started at Grantham. I had a genuine fondness for Meadow Lane from my two spells as a player there, and a call from Roy Parker seemed to be a Godsend. I knew Roy as a director at Leicester, and now he was with Notts and a familiar voice with the message: "The manager's job has become available at Notts, would you be interested?"

I knew this was going to be difficult. I'm not naïve and I took on board the wisdom of folk who said the timing of a job is important – the right job can come at the wrong time.

It's fair to say I was warned about the task I was taking on. Notts were a new beast now my friend Derek Pavis had gone, and they had been taken over by a supporters' trust with Steve Thompson as acting chairman. Also, the team was struggling near the bottom of League One.

When I met Steve Thompson, he said he wanted me in the job and wasn't going to interview anyone else. There was a great emotional pull for me to take it. I still lived in the Nottingham area and the club meant a great deal to me. From the moment I started as a manager, I always wanted to manage in the Football League and go as high as possible. If I turned down the chance to manage Notts County now, for all their problems, there was no guarantee the job would come my way again. Add to that, the fact I had promised Darron we would work at Meadow Lane together.

Talking of Darron, he had done a fantastic job at Tamworth. I was so proud of him. He had got the club promoted to the Conference and I watched them in the FA Trophy final at Villa Park when they lost 2-0 to Burscough.

When I took the job, I noted Notts had got rid of 12 managers in the last 12 years, and I told Mr Thompson I didn't want to be number 13.

One way or another, this was our job. I shook hands on the deal, Darron came with me as assistant manager, and I believed for the best. I was aware of the problems, but confident of who I was as a manager, now with a fair bit of experience, and ready to give it everything to keep Notts County up.

Things started to unravel quickly. I was surprised to find a professional team didn't have a place of its own to train. This meant an often-daily problem of trying to book venues such as Gedling Town, or Boots, or train down beside the Trent. It wasn't the best start to a day when secretary Tony Cuthbert said we were struggling to find anywhere to go.

The chairman then told me we needed to cut the playing budget. He hadn't mentioned this at the interview and this was the last thing I wanted to hear when we were struggling for our lives. Altogether the club was begging, stealing, and borrowing at a time making it difficult to keep the players on track.

There was one short spell when results started to turn for us. First, we had a fine 2-1 win at Brentford. I remember that game because of Darren Caskey, or Cask as I know him, who was arguably our most talented player. Cask looked a bit lost and was having problems with his discipline, leading me to have a go at him before kick off. I had never seen a professional player with so much mud on his boots and told him he was a disgrace. To his credit, Cask responded by putting on one of his best performances in a Notts shirt and was quick to tell me it wasn't the boots, but the player wearing them that counts. He was outstanding.

That gave us a chance to claw ourselves out of the relegation zone for the first time in months, which we did with victory over

Grimsby. I felt I had the players in the right place before the home game on the Saturday against leaders Plymouth.

The build up to that all-important clash was marred by a phone call from an agent representing striker Paul Heffernan, another of our better players. He told me a deal had already been agreed to move Heffs on to another club in the summer. I knew his contract was up and couldn't do anything until the end of the season. It disgusted me that the agent threw that spanner into the works, perhaps trying to prompt me to offer his client better terms, when we were in such a precarious position.

We played very well against Plymouth and should have won. Our big chance came when we won a penalty and Heffs missed it. Coincidence, of course, but I couldn't help but remember the conversation. The game finished 0-0 and one point instead of three turned out to be the beginning of the end.

We never reached the same level again and ultimately finished well short of survival. History repeated itself for me at Notts. I suffered my first and only relegation as a player at Meadow Lane and now it happened as a manager. It was my job to do something about it.

I needed to reshape the squad to make us a force in League Two on a reduced budget. The problem was brought into focus when flamboyant agent Eric Hall came to talk about Cask. Boy, was meeting him an experience of its own. He told me Cask was this and that and what he could do for us – all of which I knew anyway – and we needed to offer him a new, better deal. Sadly, I had to tell him I couldn't. We didn't have the cash and Cask hadn't generally been at his best.

It was a big summer off the field too. After a lot of hard work and searching, I secured a permanent training facility at Nottingham University to ease some of our problems. It was also a venue where we could have lunch after training, so I could ensure the players were eating properly. Darron and I also cleared out the old changing rooms behind the goal so we could store our training kit. Sounds like a small job, but it helped us out massively.

Everything I did whilst I was at Meadow Lane was with the best of intentions. Watching the youth team at Nottingham University, I was very impressed with David McGoldrick, then a 16-year-old schoolboy. I told the academy staff I wanted him to train with the first team and got some criticism for giving him his debut at Bournemouth. But I saw something in him and he made Notts some money when he later went to Southampton. He has been in the Premier League with Sheffield United the last two seasons.

Another youngster I promoted was Kelvin Wilson, who scored an own goal on his debut at Brighton. He eventually went to Preston and had a good career with Forest and Celtic.

I was interested in the youngsters in the academy. Interested enough to save some parents time and money. I spoke with the coaches about all the youngsters and was surprised and disappointed when they were adamant that only a few of them had any chance of making it. I got stick from parents for scrapping the under 11s, 13s, and 15s, and telling the coaches to promote the promising lads into higher age groups. But I did it because parents were bringing their youngsters to us at great cost, not knowing their lads had already been written off.

I accept my recruitment didn't work out. I brought in players who didn't come up to the mark. The result was a poor start to our League Two campaign, not helped by a series of injuries. On the eve of the trip to Rushden and Diamonds, I didn't have a fit centre back and asked the chairman for funds to bring in a defender or two. The answer was no and, with round pegs in square holes, we got hammered 5-0.

When we returned for training, club secretary Tony Cuthbert said I needed to attend a meeting in the boardroom. I thought nothing of it until I went through the door and saw the secretary sitting there. Then I realised something was about to happen.

I could have accepted that, I really could. I had worked very hard, but results hadn't improved. It was November and instead of a promotion challenge, we were struggling at the wrong end of the table. But I will never accept the way they did it.

I could have done with Derek Pavis still being at Notts. The only ally I had in that meeting was Roy Parker as Steve Thompson said how unacceptable our situation was. He was sacking me as manager but said they would 'find me another job'. What the hell did that mean? I told them I was a football manager and didn't want 'another job'.

This was the first time I had been sacked. This is not a 'woe is me' story. I took the job in January when we were in big trouble and was gone by November when the new season had only just started.

I spent the next few days at home before getting a call to say I needed to report back to Meadow Lane. I got in touch with my friend John Barnwell, from the League Managers' Association, and he advised me to do what Notts said whilst they looked at my contract. There was possibly some wording in there I wasn't aware of.

It was obvious what Notts were doing. They were trying everything not to pay me compensation. I had signed a three-year contract and left before the first one was over. Perhaps they couldn't afford to pay off yet another manager.

Driving back into Meadow Lane was a weird, weird feeling. I was sat in the foyer waiting when Tony Cuthbert walked in. I had a great working relationship with Tony so asked him what I was supposed to be doing. "I don't know, Gary," he said. The whole thing was so embarrassing, belittling. Half an hour later Tony walked back in, handed me a notepad and pen and told me to develop a new youth system. It felt like they had made this job description up on the spot.

I walked through the main office and into a room at the back. Others were busily going about their daily work. I didn't know what to do. My hours were 9am to 5pm with an hour's lunch break. I spent the morning writing nothing, had lunch, wrote nothing in the afternoon, and went home. This nonsense went on for a couple of weeks. I knew in my heart of hearts it didn't matter a jot what I did or didn't do.

The club appointed one of my players Ian Richardson as caretaker manager. I had no contact, either with him, or any of the players. The closest I came to normal life was when Steve Sutton, whom I had taken on as goalkeeping coach, slipped a piece of paper through the door saying 'we have got a plan for you to escape'. I appreciated his humour. It was a rare moment of light in the darkness.

Don't get me wrong, this was a very, very tough time. I may have lost football matches but didn't deserve to be treated like this. A club I cared a lot about was doing its best to force me to resign – or that's how it felt.

Finally, I went to my doctor and he signed me off. I hadn't suffered from depression before, but I was starting to feel worthless. I was losing my self-belief and generally in a bad place. I was getting up in the middle of the night finding it hard to sleep.

The issue was resolved when Notts invited me back for a meeting and sorted out a financial settlement. I wish they'd have been honest enough to do that before. But better late than never.

I don't think football fans realise the effect losing your job as a manager can have on your life. This was probably made worse for me because I lived locally. I started to feel nervous walking into a shop in case someone recognised me as the former manager of Notts County.

The criticism from Notts didn't stop. I saw comments indicating the club's troubles started with Gary Mills. I know that wasn't fair. Nobody could fault me for the hard work and effort I put in at Notts. But I've been in football long enough and am honest enough to know it's results that count.

I can't emphasise enough how dark a place the way I was treated by those officials at Notts County took me to. This had never happened before, or since, during my time in football.

I still have a great fondness for Notts as a club. They mean a great deal to me after the two spells I spent at Meadow Lane as a player, but I'm referring specifically to chairman Steve Thompson and his board. The way they dealt with me was nothing short of a disgrace. Anyone who knows me will vouch for the fact I deserve to be treated with respect and in a proper manner.

Regardless of what was happening at Notts, I got a lot of pleasure watching my son Ryan progressing and developing in his rugby career. It was a great moment when he received a letter asking him to attend a get together for England under 19s at Loughborough University. Sadly his career was later blighted by injury.

Also during this time I received the very sad news that my old gaffer Brian Clough had passed away at the age of 69.

I was at training when I was told and, although I was aware he was unwell, it still came as a shock. He wasn't a blood relative, but the Gaffer meant a lot to me. He played a massive part in my life in helping me to become the man I was. It's a weird feeling because you feel people like that are always going to be there.

I took phone calls and requests for interviews as the news began to sink in. But it was after my dismissal at Notts two or three months later that one of the lessons the Gaffer taught me helped pull me out of my brief depression.

I took a leaf out of his book when Sue and I decided to go to Sharm El Sheikh in Egypt for a week's holiday. He was renowned for taking us on short breaks to give us a physical and emotional break, and this was what I needed in my hour of need.

Although not a great reader, I took Brian Clough's autobiography with me. It was a lovely, relaxing time with my wife, and on the beach, reliving those wonderful memories. Reminding myself of the Gaffer's wisdom did me a world of good.

The experience at Notts briefly made me doubt whether I was suited to being a football manager, and whether I wanted another club. But, as a very positive person, I soon found myself coming round and regaining my sense of perspective.

I told Sue I was now fine and wanted to get back into management again. She asked whether I was sure, and I said 'yes', I was. I could see in her face she was pleased I was back to my normal self. As always, my wife came through for me when I needed her most. Now we could look forward to the next chapter.

CHAPTER 10
THE BEST AND SADDEST
OF TIMES

By BUSTER BELFORD, kit man for Tamworth FC for 30 years

GARY, or the gaffer as I still call him, turned this club round. He was the best manager I've worked with at Tamworth during his two spells with us.

He taught us about being professional. He told us we were all a team and referred to us as his family. Gary got the players to open up and we all enjoyed working with him.

On one away trip Smudger (Adrian Smith) was struggling to sleep, so Gary invited him down and bought him a couple of pints of Guinness. Gary and Smudger played a blinder next day.

He taught us to play attractive football, passing it rather than kicking it long. We were competing during Gary's time with big clubs on much bigger budgets, some of which are near the top of League Two today.

It's in Gary's blood to be successful. Finishing 16th in the Conference Premier was a superb achievement for Tamworth, one of the best in our history.

Had he stayed longer we could have gone even further, but he couldn't turn down clubs such as Coventry City and York City.

I sometimes go to York and their fans, too, say how brilliant Gary was for them.

He's a great guy, from a lovely family, who has never forgotten his roots.

*****

I LEFT Notts in November 2004 and was appointed manager of Alfreton Town in May 2005. I'd applied unsuccessfully for two or three jobs before the chance came out of the blue.

I was watching my daughter Ria playing girls' football – she was a true midfield dynamo – when I was told the job was becoming available up the road.

Ideally after starting off in management in Non-League and then going to Notts, I would have preferred to stay in the Football League. But Alfreton were in the Conference North, a league I already knew a good deal about, and within convenient travelling distance. I felt right about giving it a go and submitted my application.

Alfreton chairman, Wayne Bradley, invited me for an interview and 24 hours later he phoned back to offer me the job. I must have thanked him a dozen times, I was so thankful. It was great to feel wanted again after what happened at Meadow Lane.

My first call was to Darron Gee. He had shared my dream of working at Notts County and the way we left Meadow Lane had been a kick in the teeth for him. I was delighted to call him with the good news we were back in business, and he once again became my assistant manager.

The league season had just finished and I signed a three-year contract. We had a decent budget, albeit mostly taken up by players we already had on contract, and I felt I had the bit between my teeth from word go.

There was a feel-good atmosphere about Alfreton Town Football Club, not least created by the chairman. Wayne took huge pride in the club and still does to this day. He wanted things done right and I got on great with him from day one. Unfortunately, results weren't as good as either of us had hoped in my first season, but he never put my job under any pressure.

I didn't go to Alfreton as player manager but ended up playing regularly for them. I had thought my playing days were over after being at Coventry and Notts but signed at the Impact Arena in case I was needed.

I began playing regularly in the first season and continued into my second. I started at right back, or in central midfield, and thoroughly enjoyed the chance to play Conference football at the age of 46. Ok, Darron had to hold my number up and substitute me every now and again, but that was the exception rather than the rule. I still felt very fit.

There were a few problems as with most Non-League clubs. Gettiing onto the pitch to train was rare in winter due to water on the surface. Sometimes we settled for a game of darts and some banter which wasn't ideal preparation.

The weather got the better of us was when we were due to entertain Kettering Town. This was due to be Paul Gascoigne's first game as manager. For obvious reasons, there was a lot of media interest, including Sky Sports. Unfortunately, it rained all day and I realised the game was likely to be called off.

The teams were in their dressing rooms when I was asked to go onto the pitch with the referee and Gazza. I introduced myself to the former England star and realised immediately he was the worse for wear. The referee told us there was no way the game could go ahead, but Gazza was having none of it. He took the ball from the official and tried to dribble up the pitch with it, shouting 'we've played in worse than this, Millsy, let's get the game on'. But there was no way that was going to happen, so Gazza settled for a drink at the bar with me instead before he went off in the team bus.

The budget was cut by more than 50 per cent towards the end of the season as the chairman tightened his belt. This was very understandable but made my task that much harder.

I was with Alfreton until the January of the following season and had no intention of leaving before my old club Tamworth came calling. Wayne pulled me in and said Tamworth had made an official approach, but he didn't want me to go. Nevertheless, this was very appealing for me due to the great times I had enjoyed at The Lamb, and the fact they were in the Conference Premier

I also liked the idea of taking charge of a full-time club again and training day in day out. The fact they were struggling against relegation didn't faze me. I felt sad about leaving Alfreton and remain grateful for the opportunity and the confidence Wayne, in particular, had in me.

Compensation was agreed and I was soon reintroducing myself to familiar, friendly faces. It was great to see Buster Belford, the club's kit man, again, and the feeling was mutual. Characters such as him make working in Non-League football so enjoyable.

We had a lot of fun together and I know Buster will smile at a couple of memories I'm sharing. On an away trip, the hotel receptionist warned me about the key card. She said it was important not to let it get in contact with our mobile phones because it could deactivate it. I passed this information on to Buster and the rest of the lads. Buster's reaction was to pull his phone out of his pocket, make a call and announce triumphantly to the rest of us: "It's still working!"

"Not your phone, your room card," I told him. You couldn't make it up.

The other was when hard working Buster was looking forward to his end-of-season holiday in Tenerife, a place he liked to go to. We were on our way to Salisbury for an FA Trophy quarter final when he told me he had booked his next trip for May 10. "Hold on," I replied. "The FA Trophy final is on May 20!" That started banter between me, Buster, and the players, as I used it to motivate them in the pre-match team talk. I said something on the lines that even Buster expected us to lose, so we better prove him wrong. When the game started, Salisbury scored in the first minute and, as I turned round in anguish, I swear I saw Buster Belford punching the air! He needn't have worried about changing his booking because we were beat 3-0.

Overall, we had a good team behind the scenes at The Lamb and they knew the way I worked. I was the manager but was neither above nor below them. Everyone knew their jobs and it was important all of us did them well.

Sadly, we couldn't keep Tamworth in the Conference Premier. It was a fairly similar situation as at Notts. But, although I was disappointed, it didn't put me on the back foot. Instead, I was determined to make the club better and get them back up straightaway, if possible.

I talked with Darron that summer about the strategy. I was looking for experienced players I either knew, or knew of, to turn things round quickly. Recruitment is a massive issue for any football club and I had to think long and hard about who to sign.

Not everything went right. It was me who persuaded Gerry Taggart to come to us after playing with him in Leicester City Legends matches. At first, the Northern Irishman, a popular and dependable defender at Leicester, wasn't sure, but eventually the idea of playing full time again was too good to resist.

Unfortunately, it didn't work out for Gerry, who found it tougher than he thought, and we had to cut his time short. That wasn't easy, particularly dealing with a colleague and friend. The fact Gerry then got a job at Leicester City softened the blow.

Things didn't work out for Tony Thorpe, another experienced player I knew from Leicester City. One afternoon he took the ball round the goalkeeper and then placed his shot wide. Speaking with him about his bad miss, he admitted he was having problems with his eyesight!

We finished about halfway in Conference North that season which meant a change of direction as we looked forward to 2009/10. This time Darron and I spoke about recruiting younger players and we put together an unbelievable side.

We got the squad together for a pre-season tour of Ireland and could see the spirit was developing. The lads were exceptional. They were smiling, looking forward to coming to training, and everything seemed right.

There were some unexpected moments that made us laugh. The first was caused by Trevor Benjamin, the former Leicester City striker. He played a few games for us but his debut at Hayes and Yeading is the one I remember best. The lads were out on the pitch warming up when I noticed Trevor wasn't with us. So, I asked Buster to go back into our dressing room and tell him to get a shift on.

Buster reported no sign of our new striker. Where on earth had he got to? Then we realised that, for reasons only known to him, he was running across the pitch warming up with the Hayes and Yeading players!

Another off-beat moment came when we stopped near Stoke for a pre-match meal on the way to an away trip. The lads were dressed in their tracksuits with club badges and Darron and I noted there was another young man eating with us.

I thought he was a friend of one of the players and decided not to say anything until later. As for the players, perhaps they thought we had signed a new player. Who knows?

Anyway, the mystery was solved when a coach pulled up outside carrying the Stafford Rangers team. The unidentified young man was one of their players who had somehow blagged a free meal with us!

That was a terrific season and we achieved our mission by winning the league and gaining promotion back to the Conference Premier. I was also delighted to be voted Conference North Manager of the Year. I was so happy with the team that I didn't have to make major signings for the step up. We finished 16th in our first campaign in the higher league, which sounds unspectacular but was a fair achievement for us.

My second spell at Tamworth, which proved extremely happy and successful on the field, was mixed with extremely sad events in my family.

Dad had to stop watching the matches due to his fast deteriorating health. It meant so much that Mum, Dad, and Polly followed me anywhere and everywhere throughout my playing and managerial career. Polly picked them up and together they barely missed a match.

Mum was my biggest fan. It didn't matter how I played, she always told me how good I was and defended me against anyone who said otherwise. I always knew in my heart of hearts when I didn't play well, but that's why I love my Mum. Dad, on the other hand, would be more honest about my performances.

After he was diagnosed with lung cancer, I continued to visit my parents weekly and one day he invited me into the back garden. There he told me he didn't intend to take the recommended course of chemotherapy. I was upset because, at 74, he potentially had years to live. In the end he decided to have the chemo and was then told he needed radiotherapy. This consisted of 28 sessions, each of which I took him to hospital for.

We noticed he was becoming slower and more confused and eventually he was diagnosed with dementia. Mum looked after him as long as she could until there was no real choice but for him to go into a home. I'm not a churchgoer, but I was praying in my way for my Dad.

Things went downhill when he had a fall and ended up in hospital, where I was given the very sad news that 'your Dad has only got a few days to live'. I told Darron I couldn't attend training for a while. Dad was a fighter and never gave in and we all wanted to be as close to him as possible in his last days.

The end came after Mum told me to go to training. I drove into the ground on the Monday morning and was in the dressing room when I got a call from the nurse, 'you need to get to the hospital as quickly as possible'. I drove back along the M6 but was too late. By the time I got to hospital, Dad had passed away.

This was a very difficult time for me and I still have questions which will probably never be answered. Did the radiotherapy make his condition worse? I don't know. Regarding the dementia, Dad played at a time of the heavy leather balls. There is a lot of publicity and awareness today about possible damage caused by heading a football. Again, I will never know whether this caused Dad's illness.

Tamworth had an away game the following evening and Mum told me best thing was to do my job. Geebo was warming the team up whilst Buster and I stood on the pitch. Naturally, I was thinking about Dad when a white feather fell onto the grass. Being a bit superstitious, I picked it up the feather and keep it in my wallet to this day.

I miss Dad dearly, but it was some consolation for me when I decided to visit him at the funeral directors. He looked so beautiful, at peace. The church was packed for his funeral in Northampton. Everyone stood to applaud Dad. It still gives me the shivers when I recall how much he meant to everyone at the football club.

Only a couple of months later – on April 24, 2010 – my playing career finally came to an end. I started in the 4-3 defeat at home to Ebbsfleet before being substituted for the former Forest defender Des Lyttle in the 55th minute. I was 48 years and five months old.

We were flying, and second in the Conference during the opening stages of the 2010/11 season, before my career took another surprise change of direction.

CHAPTER 11
YES, YES, MINSTER!

STEVE Greaves is a great mate, and I was delighted to be best man at his wedding in Nottingham – but he'll forgive me for this confession. Most in my position spend the day fretting over their speech, whilst part of me was thinking about what I'd soon be saying to York City owner Jason McGill.

Sue and I were on our way to the wedding when I took a phone call, "Would you be interested in becoming manager of my football club?" he asked.

I told him about the bad timing. I couldn't talk there and then, but the answer was 'yes'. I was more than interested in working for York City Football Club and politely asked Jason to ring back the next day.

Steve will know why that phone call went round and round in my mind. That's because he is a massive Notts County supporter. Football is in his blood and that's the way things work. It's very difficult to block the game out of your head no matter what you are doing.

Leaving Tamworth was the last thing I expected. I had a great relationship with Bob Andrews and enjoyed almost every second of my two spells there. In addition, the team Darron and I had put together was going like a train back in the Conference Premier.

But York City are a big football club. When I began my playing career with Forest, they were also in Division Two. They had been in the Football League for 75 years until being relegated to the Conference in 2003/4.

It didn't take a genius to work out how important it was to the club and the people of York to regain that status. Eight years on and, like several famous clubs before and since, they were becoming part of the Non-League furniture. I felt privileged Jason may be putting his faith in me to restore their fortunes.

The move had to be done right. When Jason phoned back, I insisted he spoke with Tamworth before we got together. Again, Tamworth kindly didn't stand in my way. Next Lee Philpott, my former Leicester teammate and now my agent, came with me to York to meet the chairman.

Jason McGill explained that York City was now a family-run club with his father Rob and sister Sophie also heavily involved. We talked for an hour and it appeared to be going fine. Then when I asked about the salary, Jason McGill instantly closed the meeting down. That confused Lee and I when we chatted about it on the way home. It felt like the job had gone and I didn't know why. Clearly, I had to sort out the finances to leave a full-time job at Tamworth. But within 24 hours all became clear.

Jason phoned Lee about the contract and to invite me back to York to finalise the deal. Sure enough, Jason offered me the job and I felt a million dollars. But there were a couple of issues to sort out. I didn't fancy a two-hour daily trip from Nottingham to York, and I wanted Darron as my full-time assistant. He had a job with a security firm but came to an agreement with them to join me at York. My travel issue was sorted as they offered me use of an apartment in the city, which was something novel for me.

Jason and his father showed us round the ground, training facilities, and the apartment. The chairman was adamant I was the man to take York City back to the Football League. He invited me to shake his hand on the deal with the contract being drawn up the following day. My hand went across that table in a flash with the biggest smile on my face.

I was instantly looking forward to the job. The fact it was already halfway through October and York were nearer the bottom end of the Conference didn't faze me. Infact the opposite. Taking on a struggling club brought out the best in me as a manager. York City felt like the right club for Gary Mills – this was going to be a massive challenge, but one I was ready for.

I drove back home that night to tell Sue I was taking the job before going back to York to take training on the Thursday. That first meeting with the players was all-important to me, and one reason why I always like to work with an assistant.

I get so much from that first contact. Darron is another pair of eyes and ears to discover who is listening to me and who isn't. I am always true to myself because the players need to know what kind of person I am. I know I talk to people in the right way, and anyone who has played for me will tell you I'm respectful and honest. I expect the same in return. Darron confirmed my thoughts. Overall, this was a good group of lads, but those who didn't pay attention didn't stay long.

Then it was my first small-sided game - eight versus eight. I showed my players I liked to keep things simple and wanted them to work with a smile on their faces. The training facilities at York were excellent, another thing I wasn't used to. For the first time in my managerial career, it felt like a step up. York's set up was second to none and a culture shock after what I experienced at Notts, where we had to beg and borrow for somewhere to train. Darron and I went for a walk that night to see the city of York, have a meal in a restaurant, and chat like excited teenagers.

My first game, in front of our own fans against Bath City, ended in a draw. Not bad for me as, unlike many managers who enjoy the so-called bounce effect, I had never won my first match.

I was already enjoying my new surroundings. Having the apartment meant I didn't have to worry about time. Sue stayed with me at weekends and together we got to know a beautiful city, as well as a fantastic football club. When I needed to clear my mind, I took a walk around the city wall. I met fantastic people and started to make really good friends.

Working with a very hands-on chairman in Jason was a new for me, but enjoyable all the same. He was at the ground every day and involved himself in all that was going on. When I signed a new player, he took them out for a bite to eat. He was very enthusiastic and friendly. Infact I really liked him.

The rest of the staff were great too. Kit man Rob Batty couldn't do enough for me, youth team manager Steve Torpey was doing a great job and Jeff, the physio, had been there almost before the club existed. Altogether they bought into what I wanted to do and were part and parcel of our success as a group. All I asked of the staff was to do their jobs because their contribution was as important as anyone else's.

I was the same with the players. I enjoyed taking them for a walk around York – some hadn't walked around the wall before – and occasionally to the pub for a pint. This was a shock to some, but they soon started to enjoy the way I worked. I was seeking to relax them and find out more about them at the same time.

My first big decision was when Luton Town came in for midfielder Alex Lawless and defender David McGurk. Mention Luton to York fans and they shudder – there's history there and they don't get on. But this was business. They offered £80,000 for the two players, big money at that level. Both knocked at my door and asked to go. But what was best for York City?

I'd only seen both lads play a couple of times but stuck with a general principle. I knew we needed to be right defensively and replacing McGurk would be more difficult than finding another midfielder. So, I let Lawless leave and told McGurk he was going nowhere. Neither he nor his agent were happy. Luton offered a potential return to the Football League although, as a Conference club, they were no better placed to do so than us. David's agent couldn't believe I was unwilling to let his man move on. But I stuck with my guns and told David he could get back into the Football League with York City.

We only lost one of my first nine league games and the FA Cup saw our most eye-catching early results, helping to forge our great team spirit. Beating League Two leaders Rotherham United 3-0 in a first round replay after a draw at the Don Valley Stadium was great, then seeing off Darlington 2-0 helped me become Conference Manager of the Month for November.

That victory also allowed me to further bond us together. The FA Cup third round draw used to be a must for all football folk, and I ensured we got together in a social setting on the Monday evening at the club to listen to it. That's the round where lower league clubs dream of landing Manchester United or Liverpool, and a tie at Premier Division Bolton Wanderers wasn't far off.

Boy, did we play well that day. As the tie went into its closing stages, I genuinely believed we could win. Nearly 5,000 fans – double our usual home crowd – roared us on against Owen Coyle's side, four divisions higher. We had a couple of great chances late on and it took Bolton until the 83rd minute to break us down when former England international Kevin Davies smashed one into the top corner. A second goal at the end put gloss on the scoreline, but Bolton knew they had been in a real fight. When the final whistle went, it almost felt like a victory because we were starting, as a club and as a team, to become a force.

I brought in a couple of players and a good run gave us a realistic shot at the play offs. Ironically, my old club Tamworth ended that hope by beating us 2-1 at Bootham Crescent as we eventually finished 8th.

My good relationship with Jason was highlighted by the fact he took Sue and I to Spain for a few days where we enjoyed a break and discussed bringing in new players. Altogether I brought in 11 new signings that summer and very nearly landed a dream combination up front.

First striker on my shopping list was Jason Walker who impressed me playing for Barrow against Tamworth. Prising him away from Luton, who slapped a £100,000 price tag on him, seemed hard. But we found out he had a clause in his contract enabling him to leave for £60,000 and the chairman backed me. I wanted to partner Jason with a young Jamie Vardy, then playing at Halifax. But £50,000 priced us out of the market for a player who has become a Premier League star and won caps for England.

We strengthened our midfield with Matty Blair, son of Aston Villa European Cup winner Andy, Andre Boucaud, a top player with the ball at his feet, Paddy McLaughlin of Newcastle United, and Adriano Moke from Glenn Hoddle's Spanish academy.

I was grateful to the chairman for allowing us to bed in the new additions with a pre-season trip to one of my favourite places, Barnsdale Country Club. This was to foster the spirit and togetherness that became such a feature of my time at York. I felt the players were working hard and knew I had no problem with any of them. After a couple of friendlies against my old club Granthan Town and Quorn, I could almost smell we had a good team.

After our trip and pre-season form, we were more than ready for the start of the Conference season at Ebbsfleet, where we confirmed those positive vibes with the manner of our victory. One nil down in the 80th minute, debut boy Jason Walker grabbed a couple of goals.

Yes, there were the usual ups and downs, but we always looked like we had a goal in us. Braintree were hit for six, we smashed

12 past Kettering in two games, and Jason Walker netted a Wayne Rooney-style bicycle kick against Grimsby.

Our glory ride to Wembley in the FA Trophy nearly ended before it begun. I brought off Andre Boucard when we were a goal down early on to Solihull Moors, and we eventually scrambled a 93rd minute equaliser. That moment kickstarted our great run. Grimsby, going well in the league, were a big challenge in the quarter final where Scott Kerr netted his first goal in the 83rd minute to edge us to victory.

It was around this time – end of February, beginning of March – when everyone sensed what was possible. We were inside the play off frame – and a two-legged semi final from Wembley in the Trophy.

Beating Luton 1-0 at home left me with a weird feeling. Luton finished with nine men and I sensed they still regarded themselves favourites going back to Kenilworth Road. If so, they underestimated us. Luton scored first before Jamal Fyfield produced an unbelievable left foot cross in the 90th minute for Matty Blair to head us to Wembley. This was the first time in my managerial career I had taken a team to the national stadium - what a great feeling.

Losing David McGurk through injury was a blow, so I signed Chris Doig, an experienced defender I knew from Forest. Bringing in Ben Gibson, currently a Premier League defender, was an even bigger coup.

The loan move happened two or three months before the end of the season when I took a side to play Middlesbrough Under 21s. I asked former Forest teammate Mark Proctor if I could take Ben for a few games. Mark said he would ask and the answer came back no. Yet a few days later, Mark rang back to say Ben was now happy to get some game time. Ben was sent off in our 1-0 defeat at Cambridge before returning to play his part in getting us to Wembley twice. He was a very handy man to have in the crucial last few weeks of the season.

Replacing our reliable goalkeeper Michael Ingham when he got injured was more difficult as we didn't have another goalkeeper on the staff. That's when I turned to our 43-year-old goalkeeping coach Paul Musselwhite. I phoned Muzzy on the Sunday while he was tucking into his lunch. "Don't eat too many roast potatoes, mate, we need you to play at Cambridge on Tuesday night!" His answer was exactly what I wanted to hear: "No problem."

Muzzy did a great job keeping three successive clean sheets, including a 1-0 win at Braintree where a late goal by Eric Tanne, on loan from Sheffield United, secured our play off spot. It didn't bother me who our opponents were but another late goal from Adriano Moke against Forest Green meant we faced Mansfield rather than Wrexham.

With Michael Ingham now fit, we thanked Muzzy very much and left him to eat his potatoes in peace. Now it was dawning what a massive tie this was against Mansfield, yet another former Football League club desperate to go back up.

More than 6,000 people saw us draw 1-1 at Bootham Crescent before we got a predictably unfriendly welcome at Field Mill. One light bulb in the dressing room meant the lads could barely see to change, but I wasn't going to let this wind us up. So, I saved my comments for after Matty Blair nodded the winner in the 111th minute.

The finals were on successive weekends. That meant an exciting, and tense time for me and York City – it was incredible! Time to take another leaf out of my former gaffer's book in how we prepared.

I took us down south a couple of days before the final. We stayed in the lovely surroundings of the Sopwell House Hotel, a venue used by the England national team. There was some training, but also time to relax minds and bodies rather than worry about Newport County and a huge occasion.

I knew what lay ahead for my players. There are big wide eyes in that tunnel before hearing the roar of the crowd, and even the best of players can freeze. Some will question my preparation but, for me, managing anxiety and nerves was as vital as picking the team.

I opted against having a tour of Wembley the day before the Trophy final as this may have heightened any tensions, and instead opted for more team bonding. We trained in the morning, then drove into the middle of London. As we got off the coach, I gave skipper Chris Smith a few hundred quid to split between the rest of the team. The lads went their way, me and my staff went another. The order was to have a pint of Guinness or two and meet back on the bus in a couple of hours. It was a lovely way to spend a sunny afternoon.

We arrived at the stadium in our new tracksuits, Newport went the full hog dressed in their Wembley suits. That's the way I wanted it. But, despite my efforts, I saw the nervous tension in some of the lads before kick off and we started slowly before dragging our way back into the match. Our 100th goal of the season arrived in the 65th minute through Matty Blair's lob, then Laurie Oyebanjo made it 2-0.

That was York City's first triumph in a national competition and we needed to celebrate. The club booked a restaurant overlooking the water in York the following day and we got a bit merry. Yet in the back of our minds, we knew our mission was only half done. It was always number one priority to get back into the Football League, so we needed to beat Luton Town the following Sunday.

Again, it was important how we managed the following week. We had the players in early in the week for a few days of training before heading back to the same hotel. Everything was happening so quickly, before what was going to be a massive game in the history of York City.

Our preparation the day before Wembley part two was very similar – short training session, before finding a pub with a garden in St Albans where we had a lovely evening. I bought the beers; Geebo bought the crisps. We laughed, told stories, shared jokes, and had a singsong to the accompaniment of a few pints of Guinness each. I turned to Darron during the evening and said, 'this is fantastic'. Luton Town never got a mention.

Darron, Muzzy, Torps, and I sat up until 2am talking team selection. Chris Doig had been a key figure in our back four before getting injured. Loyalty didn't come into it; we felt Doigy was our best pick alongside Chris Smith. After much consideration, we went with three defenders in midfield in Dan Parslow, James Meredith, and Laurie Oyebanjo, and left out Paddy McLaughlin. That was a tough, tough decision because Paddy did a good job for us.

After announcing the team, I had some 'me' time at the hotel. I wanted time on my own, even without Darron. I sat on the bridge looking at the stream, getting myself in the right place for the challenge ahead. It was a beautiful moment before having lunch and getting on the bus for Wembley.

This was also my time to set the tone. After putting up with the players' choice of music - much of which wasn't my favourite – I treated them to Dire Straits with *Money for Nothing* blasted out loud.

They say the future's orange. It looked that way when we walked out at Wembley to be greeted by 30,000 Luton fans. Yet I felt inside we could turn the famous stadium red for the sake of 8,000 York supporters.

Now I needed to earn my money. It wasn't in the plan to go a goal down straightaway, but that was when we drew on previous experience. I had full confidence from day one onwards of that season that we could fight back.

The response of my players was magnificent. Ashley Chambers equalised in the 25th minute, and Matty Blair made it 2-1 barely a minute after the break. I've watched the whole game back several times and magnificent is the right word. They all produced performances they and York City should be proud of.

Shortly after the final whistle, there was barely a hint of orange at Wembley - it was simply all red! All connected with York will remember me dropping to my knees and looking at the sky. Throughout that season, I had prayed and chatted to my dear Dad at night, and I had a routine in my office before kick off that only Darron knew of. Being quite a superstitious person, I did a somersault in the dressing room, then pointed upwards and said: "here we go, Dad." It was much the same at Wembley in our moment of celebration. I believe Dad was looking down and smiling on me.

The sense of achievement was fantastic. I was almost in my own world. After every game that season, I went across to our fans and pointed to the sky, saying 'we are going up'. Now that gesture meant something even more special.

Watching at the back of the line as skipper Chris Smith climbed those Wembley steps will stay with me forever. The celebrations were incredible. I got drowned in champagne, then tossed in the air by the players. Moments like that are why we love football so much. Even better, my family and many, many friends were there to witness those scenes.

Next day Sue and our daughter Jenna joined the celebrations on an open top bus ride from Bootham Crescent into the city. Getting on board, I had the same feeling I had at Forest, wondering if anyone would come out to support us. I needn't have worried. As we got to the bottom of Bootham Road, I began to see them. It looked like the whole of York turned out to celebrate. This was another magical moment I wanted us all to fully take in. I could see what returning to the EFL after eight long years meant to everyone.

Sophie was busy too. She had checked in with the travel agents to arrange a four-day trip to Benidorm – starting with a bus ride from the ground to the airport at 4am the following day! Some of the players were worse for wear even before we set off. It was lovely though to continue our celebrations together and gave time for me to start turning my attention to the next season.

I had a fairly clear idea about my squad. Most players were good enough, in my view, to play in the higher league. Some had clauses in their contracts guaranteeing they would be taken on if we won promotion. The first I spoke with face-to-face was Dan Parslow. I wanted him to know on day one of the trip there was a place for him at York City.

There was one extra place on that trip for my friend Woody, one of the lads on Forest's books at the same time as me. He hadn't made it as a professional footballer, but he became a good friend. He was also a bit of a character, ideal for entertaining footballers. The lads at York really took to him that season when he organised quizzes, and insisted he came with us. Jason McGill generously agreed.

I remember that trip well – but not for the right reasons. It started predictably enough with a good night out for a few drinks – make that a lot of drinks – but next day my mood changed completely.

I was alone in my room breaking down. Whether it was anxiety, I don't know. It seemed the biggest comedown after all the hard work, excitement, pressure, success, and mind games. I rang Sue and couldn't explain why I was crying. I didn't know myself. I was shaking and not well at all. Whatever was happening, I don't ever want to repeat it.

That was the end of my socialising on that trip as I stayed in my room. When the chairman and his father asked me out for a drink, I politely declined. But I didn't want to be on my own. I was having scary thoughts of jumping off the balcony and phoned Woody to ask him to stay with me. It was a weird come down after a massive, massive high.

I then went on holiday with Sue, Polly, and his wife Pam, to a place I had fallen in love with – Turkey. The beautiful hotels and food made it the perfect place for me to relax. And it wasn't just the weather that was red hot. My phone was buzzing, too, as I worked to build my squad.

There are different views about the gap between the Conference, now the National League, and League Two. In my view, it isn't massive, but there's a greater depth of quality in the EFL. I made a few new signings and started to gel them with the lads who got us promoted. I also recruited Des Lyttle, who had helped me get Tamworth promoted, as first team coach. The anticipation around the city was like one big family.

Walking into the square in the centre of York and looking round the different markets, I had a lovely surprise. A guy was selling tankards marking York City's double triumph. They were complete with names and scores from the play off and Trophy finals. I bought two – one for myself, one for the chairman. I thought he would be as thrilled as I was. But he looked at it and said: 'where's my name?' It felt like he didn't want the gift because his name wasn't on the tankard. This was the first time I sensed a change in Jason McGill.

As you know, first games aren't my thing. Opening day promised to be a good one for our fans as we welcomed Wycombe Wanderers to Bootham Crescent. Needless to say, we lost 3-1 before picking up points regularly to get into the top ten and even the top six at one stage.

We then went on a frustrating run, drawing and losing games without playing poorly. We had injuries, too, and needed another centre back. Watching Soccer AM proved a good move as I listened to Clarke Carlisle talk about his personal problems and his desire to get back into football. I tracked him down and he agreed to come to York where he soon got himself fully fit.

The way we were playing didn't worry me, but I sensed a problem with the chairman. He wasn't the same with me as when we were in the Conference. Then he was in my office daily asking about the team, chatting, and even giving me a kiss on the cheek. Now he was much more distant. I felt after some games he was giving me the cold shoulder and asked him into my office for a chat. I pointed at my chair and said: "Do you still want me in that seat, chairman?" He said yes and denied there was any problem between us.

Before the start of the season, we agreed that, although we would love another promotion, staying in the EFL was top priority. There was no stage, even in that difficult run, when I felt we were in danger of failing.

We played particularly well at Rotherham United's new New York Stadium on a Tuesday night. Facing a side in the top three, we were good value for our 1-0 lead until they equalised in the 94th minute. I sank to my knees when that goal went in. That was a low blow.

Next up was Bradford City at Bootham Crescent, and again we played well. We had our chances, then fell behind with about five minutes left. It ended 2-0 to Bradford but Darron and I were still upbeat. We were 17th in the table. Nobody was keener than us to get that elusive win, and we knew it was coming.

Then Jason McGill, his father, and Sophie, walked in and asked Darron to leave us alone. It didn't take a genius to work out what was going to happen. The meeting barely lasted two minutes and was very matter of fact. "Gary, we are going to have to take the job away from you – unfortunately, you are no longer the manager of York City!" It was left to Sophie to thank me for the job I'd done. Secretary Lisa would sort everything out. I asked him: "Please, tell me, you haven't got someone already lined up for this seat?" The chairman wouldn't give me a straight answer.

So that was it! After all we achieved at York, I know I deserved better. I was left alone in my office – no longer my office - feeling totally shocked. Call me naïve, if you like, and, yes, I know the one certain thing when you walk into any football club as a manager is that one day you'll be walking out, but I didn't see this one coming.

Had it been handled differently; it may have softened the blow. The chairman could have been straight with me a few games earlier and told me the score. At least I would have had the chance to fight for my job.

I will go as far as saying I think Jason McGill was wrong. He had someone in charge who adored his football club and believed in those players. I knew I was still the right man for York City football club. I opened the door and asked Darron to come in. He couldn't believe it. Next person I told was my wife. Sue was in the Vice Presidents' lounge, I told her to go back to the apartment and I'd be there as soon as possible.

Some players were still at the ground. I asked the ones who had left to come back. I thanked them in the dressing room for everything they had done and said goodbye. My captain was particularly emotional. 'This isn't right' said Chris Smith, who wanted to speak with the chairman. Of course, I knew this wouldn't change anything. I had an incredible relationship with those players, but this was the end of the road.

Next it was black bag time as Sue and I cleared our things from the apartment. Sue was upset and it was a sad, sad time for me. Back in Nottingham, first on the phone was Martin O'Neill. "Be proud of what you have achieved. What they have done is scandalous," he said. Coming from him, a friend but not someone I spoke with very often, meant a hell of a lot.

Next day Sue was due to fly out to Lanzarote with her mum on holiday. She told me several times she wasn't going. She was worried about me, but I told her not to be silly and to enjoy the break. She phoned me a lot during that holiday – bless her – to make sure I was ok. My head was still spinning thinking about what might and should have happened. York City was more than just a football club to me, it was like a fairy-tale. It still is.

Darron stayed for a couple of weeks to help new manager Nigel Worthington who was appointed within 24 hours. Geebo noticed reports of the last three or four York games on the manager's desk – those weren't commissioned by me.

I expected the phone to ring. It didn't. I was out of a job again and desperate to get back in. I was at home on the last day of the season when York City ensured their Football League safety. A few players were on the phone almost straightaway, saying fans had been chanting my name.

I had a great relationship with York supporters and I wish to thank them here and now for that show of support – you will always mean the world to me.

CHAPTER 12
INCREDIBLE GATESHEAD

By GRAHAM WOOD, chairman of Gateshead FC for nine years

When Anthony Smith resigned after a shocking start to the 2013/14 season, I had only one man in mind for the manager's job – Gary Mills.

I'd followed his career as a manager and didn't need to advertise the post.

Gary then picked up the reigns for what became our most successful season to date as a Non-League club. It was by far the closest we have got to getting back in the EFL.

Losing at Wembley was such a disappointment. The way Gary set us up to play the place suited us, and I think we would have beaten Cambridge United seven times out of ten.

Gary and his assistant Darren Caskey both gave possible reasons as to why the following season didn't go so well in the league in comparison – but we enjoyed our best ever FA Cup run since reaching the quarter finals in 1953.

Gary also helped to increase public interest in our club amazingly. We were used to poor crowds in the International Stadium, but they grew and grew, leading to well over 8,000 watching us in the play off semi final against Grimsby. That was due to the type of football he played, as well as the results.

Sadly, there was a limit to what I could do. I decided it was my mission to get back into the EFL and gave it a budget of £3m. I spent more like £3.5m, and I had to step down as chairman because I couldn't afford to keep funding the club at the same level.

It was then that Wrexham came in for Gary and I couldn't stand in his way. It wouldn't have been fair on him to persuade him to stay – if anything, I advised him to move on to what is a bigger club.

My judgement of Gary was justified as his record with Gateshead was excellent. I like the guy very much and we formed a good partnership. My wife Margaret and I have remained friends with Gary and Sue ever since.

*****

By DARREN CASKEY, assistant manager at Gateshead, Wrexham, and York City

I WAS surprised how we hit it off so well when we did our A-licence together, after first playing for Gary at Notts County.

He then rang me out of the blue when I was at Ilkeston to ask me to become his assistant manager at Gateshead. I remember him telling the players we were going to make the play offs, the players' faces would have made a good picture.

Everyone was buzzing at Gateshead, and the loss in the play off final was so disappointing. It would have been amazing for the chairman if we had achieved his dream.

We enjoyed our year at Wrexham, where we finished just outside the play offs. The club was run by the supporters' club which wasn't great to deal with.

Then, he took me with him when he went back to York City and won the FA Trophy.

If you speak to 95 per cent of players who have played for Gary, they'd say they would want to play for him again. He is honest with them, and very professional. He wants them to enjoy and express themselves. Everyone likes him and the way he plays his football.

Gary has a way with people and his door is genuinely always open.

I don't think there's been a more successful manager at Conference level – Wembley was his second home for five or six years.

*****

BEING out of work for six months from March to September 2013, I began to doubt my initial optimism about getting another manager's job.

My managerial experience told me my best chance was at the end of that season. I put in plenty of applications, but only got negative replies. Even whilst enjoying our summer holiday in Cyprus, I had another disappointment. I thought Conference side Salisbury was a possibility. But again, the answer came back no.

Keeping myself involved in football only served to rub things in further. More on my experiences at a UEFA A licence course at St George's Park later, but being around managers squeezing transfer business into our very full schedule highlighted what I was missing.

There was however one big positive which served me well when I finally landed a job.

Darren Caskey told me afterwards that when he saw my name on the list of attenders, he didn't know what to expect after I'd been the manager who told him he had no future at Notts County. Now, however, we got on like a house on fire. We spent hours together talking after classroom time finally ended, sharing our experiences in professional football.

Cask is a character. In one exercise, led by former Aston Villa captain Dennis Mortimer, we were rehearsing set pieces. As the ball was delivered into the box, Cask made no attempt to track his man prompting Dennis to tell him to treat it like a real game. "I am," Cask said. "I never tracked back when I was a player!"

I was beginning to doubt I would get another chance, and thinking ahead to the October managerial casualties, when my phone rang totally out of the blue in early September. "It's Graham Wood, chairman of Gateshead Football Club – I want to speak to you about the job that has just become available as manager."

Immediately I began thinking. Gateshead had plusses - a Conference club playing at a massive stadium. On the other hand, they only attracted 300 to 400 fans creating little atmosphere. More to the point, Gateshead was a very long way from home. Twice as far as York. When I called Graham back, he invited me to meet him straightaway at The Hilton Hotel just off Junction 24 of the M1.

First impressions are important. I can honestly say, as soon as I scanned the room and Graham Wood introduced himself and said, 'pleased to meet you', I knew I would get on with him. We sat down and talked for a couple of hours. The chairman said there had already been 50 applicants but didn't want to give the job to any of them. Instead, he wanted to give it to me. Those words sent a shiver down my spine.

There were domestic issues to sort out, so I asked to sleep on my decision. It was important Sue was happy. She had developed a love for York, but neither of us knew Gateshead. I suggested we spent three or four days there to see what we thought.

Graham Wood was delighted with the idea and booked us both into the Hilton Hotel on the Tyne Bridge – the Gateshead side, of course. The journey to the northeast took three and a half hours before we were given a nice room on the fourth floor. The phone went - it was Graham checking that we'd arrived and settled in ok. "Oh, no, that's not the room, I booked you something better," he said. So, we gathered up our stuff and were redirected to an even posher room on the fifth floor including a lounge area with free food and drink. We'd been more than happy with the first room.

Graham picked us up at 7pm to take us for a lovely meal at a restaurant on the quay side at Newcastle. Now Sue was getting good vibes. Graham's talk wasn't just about football, he took a genuine interest in finding out about my wife's work and our leisure interests. After he dropped us off at the hotel, Sue commented on what a genuinely lovely man she thought he was.

Next day we went to the ground, looked at the training facilities, and were introduced to the commercial manager Grahame McDonnell who couldn't do enough for either of us. By this time, my mind was all but made up that I wanted to work at Gateshead, but Sue's reaction was the final confirmation: "I think this place is right for you."

Graham Wood was a big influence in that. But it wasn't his generous gestures that attracted me to the club, it was the passion he had for Gateshead FC.

He told me a story that, although I'd been around the game for a long time, I never really knew. I'm too young a Millsy to remember Gateshead being a Football League club, or that they

191

were controversially voted out in 1960. This history hurt Graham like it happened yesterday. He told me the club had been kicked out because of location rather than league position and replaced by Peterborough.

Although the club had folded and been reformed twice since then, it was Graham's burning desire to take them back where he felt they belonged. Like me, Graham is an emotional man and there were a few tears in his eyes when I accepted the job.

Getting in the right assistant was again vital – and geography played a part there too. Geebo said that, because of his other work commitments, he couldn't travel that far which created a problem for me in filling the assistant's role.

Who next? The chairman asked whether I could work with David Rush, the former Sunderland player, who had taken over as caretaker manager after the departure of Anthony Smith. I knew Rushy, and I was happy to do so for a short while, but I wanted to bring in my own man. And the first name that came into my mind was Darren Caskey. Problem was he was at Ilkeston Town working with Kevin Wilson and I didn't know how practical a club in the northeast was for him. When I approached Cask about the possibility of becoming my assistant and told him the club was Gateshead, he couldn't believe it. He was moving up to live in Northallerton, so this was ideal.

I thought long and hard about how to introduce myself to the players. So, I kept it simple, "Hello, lovely to meet you, I'm your new gaffer – I hope you are ready because we are going to get into the play offs!" I said. The reaction of the players was all-important – that's what I was looking for. Although it was early in the season and when I joined we were second bottom of the league, virtually everyone looked at me and listened. I knew then I'd got a good dressing room. I told them my ways in a nutshell: keep things simple, play my way, and here are half-a-dozen disciplines I expect you to follow to do your job.

My problem going into my first game at home to Hereford United was I didn't have a fit striker. Not one. So, I decided to play midfielder Josh Walker up front. We won 2-1 and Josh scored both goals. That was a great feeling and I felt at home straightaway. I could see lads with heart and ability who should have been winning more often.

Three games and three wins could have been my lot at Gateshead. Lee Philpott rang to say Forest Green Rovers, the money boys in the Conference, had come in for me. Graham Wood confirmed the approach and Lee found out Forest Green were offering to treble my wages. They would have paid me more than I earned anywhere in my football career either as a player or a manager. But there was one problem – everything was right for me at Gateshead. I got on like a house on fire with the team and the people. I told the chairman I wanted to stay and I remember him holding back a few more tears. Graham Wood had got me back into the game. He was a great man and I had already become friends with him, and Sue had formed a lovely relationship with the chairman's wife Margaret.

My relationship with Graham was great. We both enjoyed a pint and a pickled egg together occasionally in The Schooner, a pub next to the ground. Once I realised how close we were to the coast, I liked to take the players to train on the sand at a beautiful place called Tynemouth. After they finished training, I insisted they strip into their boxers and jump into the sea – even in February! Believe me, it was cold. Graham sometimes gave me some money to treat the players to fish and chips or to take us to the movies.

I was the Conference Manager of the Month in October, my first full month, and it was then I spoke with David Rush and said I was bringing in Darren Caskey. From the beginning, Cask was a different kind of assistant to Geebo, being more hands on with the training sessions. Grahame McDonnell, or GMac, as I called him, sorted me a beautiful apartment overlooking the Tyne and Newcastle United's famous St James' Park. Perfect.

Talking of location, almost all our away trips were long ones calling for me, Cask, GMac, and George Spurs, the kit man, to come up with a novel idea. We took it in turns to bring in a cheeseboard and red wine to enjoy on the coach. That was going well until GMac, bless him, brought a cheeseboard we noticed was out of date. He is now a top friend and I often remind him of that!

Our good league form was mirrored in the FA Cup, where we were drawn away to Chris Wilder's League One highflyers Oxford United in the first round proper. That was a long trip, so we agreed to travel down on the Friday with a couple of stops, which became the norm for us because of Gateshead's location. It was hammering down with rain as we approached a park in Aylesbury. I told the bus driver to stop and GMac was worried. "Are you going to get them to train in those puddles?" he asked. "No," I replied. "We're going across the road to the pub for a pint of Guinness!"

The first face I saw at the ground was my mate Alan Hodgkinson, whom I worked with at Coventry. He had been Chris Wilder's goalkeeping coach but had now come just to watch the game. Here was someone I wanted my players to meet. I introduced him to the dressing room ten minutes before kick-off, giving him the big build up. "He's a legend at Sheffield United, got into the England squad, was a coach at Rangers. . ." I was still bigging him up when Hodgy whispered in my ear: "Don't forget the MBE!"

We went 2-0 up and were playing great before Oxford hit back and finally equalised in the 90th minute. The replay at Gateshead would have been screened live on TV but was postponed and, when it was eventually played, we lost 1-0 to a penalty.

I'm always happy as a manager for people to express their honest opinions, but I make my own mind up on players. At Gateshead, I was told I would need two new centre backs. I wouldn't get anywhere with James Curtis and Ben Clark in the side. The opposite was the case. In my opinion, both could have played in the EFL – they were that good for me. James had better feet than anyone in the club.

Then there was Marcus Madison. I was told he was a nightmare to manage. I would call him a challenge. Always last for training, he walked over the hill to the training pitch at the back of the stadium with one hand down his shorts and a lollipop in his mouth. On the pitch, we needed two balls when Marcus was in the team – one for him, the other for the rest of the lads.

We had only been playing five minutes at Chester when I told Cask to get the board ready – we were taking him off! I told Marcus to stand next to me. I knew he would be angry and he probably expected a rollicking. But no. "Marcus, you are going to play in the football league one day," I said. "How can I do that if you keep taking me off?" he asked. I answered that in my office on the Monday morning. "From now on, I want you first over the

194

hill, no more lollipops and no hand down your pants, then you can become a professional footballer." Marcus Madison became almost unstoppable with us and went on to become a top player in the EFL.

That was an interesting story when I dealt with Barry Fry, the director of football at Peterborough United. Barry is a great character with his distinctive cockney accent. His approach on the phone was: "Who is this player they are all talking about at your place. You don't want any money for him, do you?"

I explained that Marcus was a big asset to Gateshead Football Club and we certainly did want a fee. Barry tried several times to persuade me to let him have our most talented player for nothing, but we eventually agreed a fee that, with add ons, amounted to £500,000 – good money for Gateshead.

There was one extra issue in the back of my mind as we approached the run in. Sue and I had booked a holiday in Turkey in May before I took the Gateshead job. That coincided with the play offs!

Despite our continued good form, that was a big ask. Cask and I calculated we needed 24 points from our last 12 games – automatic promotion form. We drew the next game at home before going to Barnet. I decided to do something different – not just playing holding midfielder John Oster up front. I'd had enough of stopping at service stations, so gave the lads the Harpole experience. We stopped to train on the sports field, where I played as a lad for Harpole Trueshots, and went for a game of skittles and a pint of Guinness (some may have had more than one) at the local, The Bull Inn, managed by a friend Alan Starmer and his wife Carol, who also provided food for us.

This was a culture shock – they had never seen the game played with three cheeses before. It's amazing, myself and Cask used to learn so much about players even when the pressure was on to knock down skittles! So, there was method in my madness – in other words, man management, even though the players had no idea. Next day we beat Barnet 1-0 with Jamie Chandler, all 5'5" of him, nodding the winner.

That winning feeling was good – and it stayed with us. We won eight, drew four, and lost none of those 12 games to finish comfortably in third to qualify for the play offs. Helping us along the way was former Forest and Chesterfield striker Jack Lester. A friend of Cask's, he joined us in February, chipped in with a few goals, and was very impressed with our football. "How come they are playing this kind of football when they don't work on it?" he asked me. "It was all down to trusting their natural ability," I said.

I had a lovely surprise towards the end of the season when invited to Craven Cottage for the league's end of season awards. Although John Still had already taken Luton to promotion, I was very proud to become Conference Manager of the Year, bringing a tear to my eye.

Gateshead fans were responding too. That initial 300 to 400 had increased to 1,500 as they enjoyed our results and our football. Now Turkey was off the immediate menu!

The first leg of our play off semi final against Grimsby Town finished 1-1. Then 8,500 watched us win the home tie 3-1 at the International Stadium. Chris Doig, then Grimsby's assistant manager, congratulated me afterwards. Then it hit me for real – we were one step away from fulfilling Graham Wood's dream.

I had taken York back into the Football League after eight years, could I now do the same thing with Gateshead after 53? I thought about my early Gateshead memories – playing there for England Schoolboys and flicking through a programme when Dad played against them for Northampton. Now history was in the making.

Not only had Gateshead never been to Wembley, I don't think any of our players had even watched a game at the national stadium, let alone played there.

It was time to learn fast. Getting to Wembley was great but, to be successful, we needed to win. We had beaten play off opponents Cambridge United, another former EFL club, 3-0 on the last day of the league season. But I'd been in the game long enough to know that didn't guarantee anything.

This was my plan: win at Wembley to clinch promotion, then the perfect celebration - surprising Sue by flying to Turkey for the last three days of the holiday.

Our preparations were like at York before both our successes at the national stadium. We had a night at Harpole for a game of skittles and more team bonding before a couple of nights at Sopwell House.

I felt so pleased for the people of Gateshead. The northeast is a hot bed of football with Newcastle United, Sunderland, and Boro grabbing all the headlines. When I joined Gateshead, we barely got a paragraph in the local newspaper. That all changed with pages and pages being written about us as we got closer to promotion. Paul Gascoigne summed up the feelings of the community when he wrote about how great it was to see Gateshead making their presence felt – and hopefully getting back into the EFL.

There was one important issue Cask and I argued about before kick off. Having led teams out at Wembley, as a player and a manager, I knew how great a thrill it was. I'd been lucky to experience it several times; this could be a one off for Cask, so I asked him to take the honour. He refused saying that I was the manager and should lead us out as usual. I was angry with him in a way but that also tells you the kind of person he is and why we get on so well.

The support we got from Gateshead at Wembley was fantastic and they saw a close game that was 0-0 at half time. It was the early stages of the second half that killed us, as Cambridge went 2-0 up before I put on Jack Lester to partner Liam Hatch up front. Jack got a goal and we piled on the pressure. We had Cambridge firmly on the back foot, but the second goal wouldn't come. Afterwards I clapped the fans, but honestly, I couldn't wait to get back down the tunnel because of the disappointment of losing.

The difference between winning and losing a play off final is massive. I had enjoyed a wonderful success at York, now it was the opposite. And this really hurt. I genuinely felt that I had let my chairman and good friend Graham Wood down at the final whistle. Not that I could have asked for any more from my players.

Cask's daughter gave me a lift to Gatwick Airport that night and I had time alone with my thoughts. Ten hours was a long time, and I seemed to be almost the only person there as I waited for my flight at 6am. I was sat there thinking 'should I have done this or that?' but now was too late to make a difference. It was a horrible time.

Eventually I arrived in Turkey and walked in on Sue at the hotel. It was lovely to see her. Sue, along with Polly, had watched the game on TV. It wasn't the celebration I planned, but a good time, nevertheless. At the end of season presentation, I apologised to the Gateshead fans for a case of so near yet so far.

There was only one thing to do – start all over again. I used my contacts with Peter Beardsley at Newcastle and Kevin Ball at Sunderland to bring in a few new players and we made a good start. We were in the top six for the majority of the first half of the season before we broke new ground in the FA Cup.

Gateshead had never been to the third round before as a Non-League club, so we wanted to make it special. As at York, I got the players together to listen to the draw. We gathered in a pub dreaming of a Premier League club – and we got one. West Bromwich Albion away.

They had appointed Tony Pulis as manager two days before the cup tie and he was staying at The Belfry, the same hotel as our players. So, I had a nice chat with Tony and his assistant David Kemp, who I played with at Seattle, the night before the game. Tony was in the stand, as he hadn't formally taken charge, yet our impressive start where we had the better of the first half hour, caused him to go down to the technical area to try to turn the tide. That happened when Albion opened the scoring five minutes before the break, and it was 2-0 by the interval which quietened our 5,000 fans.

The goals kept coming in the second half, but Tony Pulis generously came into our technical area to say how well we had played and that we didn't deserve to be six down. "We're only five down, Tony, you're not that good!" I said. At that very moment, the sixth goal went into our net. "Well, maybe you are then," I said. The game finished 7-0 which was no reflection of the way we played.

Unfortunately, we also faded away in the Conference and finished 10th. That was disappointing yet we still believed good things were round the corner. But there had been a bolt from the blue before our last game. The chairman phoned to say the club had received an approach for me from Wrexham. I told him I didn't want to go but Graham Wood's words surprised me. He advised me to leave, saying he was going at the end of the season and the club wouldn't have the same budget.

I had the ultimate respect for the chairman who put heart and soul, and finances, into Gateshead Football Club. He was telling me the opposite of what I wanted to hear, but I sensed he was thinking of my best interests. That was typical of Graham, as the chairman and my friend. But I don't think he realised how painful it was for me to leave a football club that had become so close to me. I had also grown to love the northeast so much so that Sue and I still talk about retiring there.

We lost to Martin Allen's Barnet as they clinched promotion, and I arranged to speak with Wrexham. Cask and I met with Barry Horne and Don Bircham who seemed to be the main decision makers. I didn't need reminding about a club with such a proud history, and very frustrated to be in the Conference. They also told me there would be a lot of work to do in the community as well as the first team.

I was struggling with the thought of leaving Gateshead after two incredible years, when the situation became more complicated. The chairman rang to say Tranmere Rovers, another leading Conference club, were also interested. I again told Graham Wood I preferred to stay but he said 'Gary, go'. He made it clear I needed to decide.

Tranmere chairman Mark Palios spoke with Lee and arranged a meeting with me. Meanwhile Wrexham heard about Tranmere's interest which was awkard as there was already bad feeling between the clubs.

I was shown around the ground and introduced to coaches and office staff before being told they would ring me next day. I left confused if I had been offered the job or not. Lee was told Tranmere were 90 per cent sure they wanted me but were seeing another candidate, whilst Wrexham wanted an answer to their job offer.

It was the only time in management I've been involved in a tug-of-war with three clubs. I chose Wrexham because they wanted me unconditionally. So, after Yorkshire and the northeast, I was on my travels again to Wales.

Thank you, Gateshead and the Northeast, you are special people.

CHAPTER 13
LIFE IN WALES AND
YORK REVISITED

By JON 'THE BEAST' PARKIN, YORK CITY STRIKER

WHEN my agent said Gary Mills had been in touch, it suited me to go back up north from Newport at the end of my career.

York had been where my career kickstarted but when I was told they were bottom of the Conference I knew they must be f------ shite. After my debut there when we lost at Tranmere, I realised I was right.

Millsy was good with me. He treated everyone the same, but differently – if you see what I mean. He'd tell me to go to the gym instead of training when I was struggling.

Before my second game at Dover, he asked me what I liked to do on a Friday night. I said 'have six pints' out of banter but when he took us to the pub, I was one of three players who 'over indulged'. I didn't have six, I had nine!

I played next day with a bad hangover, but it concentrated my mind on the game. I scored in the 25th minute and we drew 2-2. Afterwards, the chairman rang, and I thought I was in trouble. But he congratulated me on 'the best centre forward performance I've seen'.

There were about 25 shite players at York when I joined, but Millsy got in his players – he called us 'proper men'. We were a top six side in the second half of the season, but I'll never forget that final day against Forest Green Rovers, one of my former clubs.

I scored twice and at 2-2 we were staying up. The last 25 minutes were like a testimonial, then we got the bad news Guiseley scored.

The place was silent at the end. The Forest Green fans showed their respect.

I walked out at Wembley for the Trophy final thinking 'I don't want to be here' – particularly as I'd been due to fly to Mexico on holiday the previous day! I scored and we won. It didn't mean so much because we had been relegated but I can always say I scored at Wembley.

I'd done well scoring 16 goals and Millsy was straight with me. He said the money wouldn't be great in Conference North, but I stayed, partly out of respect for him.

It's never easy adjusting to a new league, higher or lower, and, if some of the grounds in the Conference were bad, the next league down was horrendous.

I honestly think that, if Millsy hadn't got the sack, we would have been promoted – but that's football.

I will also add this: we never lost after going to the pub on a Friday!

*****

I HAD a hint of what to expect at Wrexham talking with their previous manager Kevin Wilkin before our teams clashed at Gateshead. That was the return match after we played round Wrexham all night in a 3-0 win at The Racecourse Ground, a result and performance that may have influenced my eventual appointment. Kevin Wilkin was in the tunnel, looking like he didn't want to go out. He told me how difficult it was to manage Wrexham and I tried my best to encourage him.

I was soon made even more aware how keen the club was to succeed. Sue was there when I was introduced as manager in front of about 20 press, a lot at that level. First question was on the lines of: "Gary, do you realise the expectations at Wrexham Football Club?" I said expectations were normal and motivated, rather than worried, me. Similar questions fired at me almost smelt of desperation.

Everything at Wrexham, including the training facilities and the ground, spoke of a very big club at Conference level and I was genuinely excited to be working there. The playing budget agreed in our initial talks was, however, very similar to Gateshead's.

I began working on the usual summer decisions. Some players wanted to leave, others to stay, plus there was room in the budget to bring in new players. But, running through my transfer plans with Barry Horne, we discovered a hitch. I calculated I still had 20 per cent of my budget left to sign a couple more players, but he said I had already used it all up. Barry insisted my budget was 20 per cent less than we had agreed.

I spoke with Cask and neither of us were happy. I had signed my contract believing one thing when the real terms were different. For two or three days, I thought about walking out before deciding to put my grievance to one side and get on with my job.

An early fans forum was packed. First question was: "I hope you are not like Kevin Wilkin who bought a table tennis table rather than training the players?" I replied: "Kevin Wilkin is not only a good manager but a nice bloke and, if he has got us a table tennis table, I will use it. I like the game myself."

Immediately I got an uncomfortable message. Club officials gave me the impression they knew about my success as a Conference manager at Tamworth, York, and Gateshead, but didn't know Gary Mills or the way I worked. I was constantly being quizzed about the same methods that had brought me success.

Wrexham was run, during my time in charge, by a supporters' trust. It seemed too many people had an input which led to unnecessary added pressure. Yet there were plenty of positives. I relished the challenge of getting Wrexham back into the EFL, and I settled happily into an apartment in Chester, overlooking the river and owned by two beautiful people in Mel and Elwyn. I kept my location secret as there was no love lost between Wrexham and Chester.

I put together a competitive squad capable of doing the job. An opening day defeat at Bromley was familiar enough for me but didn't go down well with the Wrexham press. We played some great football early on, during which Wes York gave us the lead, but lost 3-1. "We haven't lost our first game in recent seasons," one reporter said. "Well, perhaps we've found why we haven't been promoted," I answered.

I had a cuppa with Wrexham legend Mickey Thomas who said he loved my comment and soon found an ally in Joey Jones –

yes, the same Joey Jones I faced in my first Central League game all those years ago. In charge of the youth team, Joey was 'old school' like me, and a lovely bloke.

The fans were happy, too, as we won our next five league games. We were passing the ball and dominating games, leading some to say they hadn't seen football like it at The Racecourse Ground for years.

We were still in the top six at Christmas, before a disappointing festive season set the scene for the second half as we finished eighth, a fair way short of the play offs. I hold my hands up and agree that wasn't good enough for Wrexham Football Club. I couldn't put my finger on why we faltered, but these things happen.

I reshaped the squad for the following season where I lasted 11 games. We had won four and drawn four when we got convincingly beaten 3-0 at Macclesfield. The fans were beginning to make their voices heard. It wasn't nice knowing some didn't want me as their manager any longer. But the end genuinely took me by surprise.

I was in Nottingham on the Thursday after the Macclesfield defeat, preparing to drive to Wales for a fan's forum. When Barry Horne phoned to say we should meet up at a hotel beforehand, I thought he wanted to run through our message to the fans. When I arrived, Barry rang to invite me upstairs to a room where he was sat with Don Bircham. Immediately, I sensed the worst.

I was told my services were no longer required which was disappointing. I thought I was worth longer than one season and 11 games but became another victim of the growing trend to change managers at Wrexham. But, no, I have no regrets. It was a privilege managing the club.

The problem was that the club seemed to constantly question my man management methods that had worked extremely well and successfully at my previous clubs. If I went back into Wrexham Football Club today, I would approach the job in the same way – that's the way I work. If I'm successful, it's because of the way I do my job. Ultimately, if I'm released from my job (sacked), then the same principle applies. As Frank Sinatra would have said, 'I did it my way'.

I didn't have time to dwell on it because my phone rang two days later. "Do you know who this is?" he said. "No, sorry," I replied. "It's Jason McGill, are you interested in coming back to York?" I wasn't expecting that!

I knew Jackie McNamara had stepped down, but I didn't think for one second that I would be his replacement. And that's about as long as it took me to say yes to a club very close to my heart.

Jason McGill wanted to see me straightaway to talk terms, with a view to take training next day before an FA Cup tie on the Monday. He also said Jackie McNamara was staying at the club in a different capacity. Sue was more than happy with the prospect of a York return; others weren't so enthusiastic. For the first time, some of my friends warned me not to take the job.

I'd only spoken with Jason McGill once since my sacking. I was watching Sunderland play Manchester United with Graham Wood when he sat in front of me. Jason remarked on me doing well at Gateshead. I didn't say much but wished I'd said 'yes, that's because I'm a good manager.'

He wasn't the reason I went back to York City. That was because of the relationship I had with the club and the fans. We met on the outskirts of the city. It felt a bit surreal seeing Jason again – particularly as Jackie McNamara was also at the meeting.

Jason said he wanted me until the end of the season; I said I wanted a better contract than that. Terms were quickly agreed before Jason made a surprise confession as Jackie went to the toilet. He asked if I knew why he had been different with me during our season in the EFL. When I said no, he said it was because I had declined to go out for a drink with him and his father in Benidorm! I couldn't believe my ears. "Chairman, you have no idea what I was going through in Benidorm," I said, telling him my story. I found his comment childish and petty. It was a shock to my system.

I had to settle in straightaway, staying in a hotel for a few weeks before the city centre apartment the chairman promised was available, and working with Steve Torpey until I got Cask in from Wrexham. I had the same office, same desk, but a lot had changed since I first walked into Bootham Crescent.

It was a great feeling taking training for the first time. I was on an emotional rollercoaster after losing my job at Wrexham, then being reappointed at York almost immediately. I had to rely heavily on Steve's advice at first as I didn't know many of the players – all but one from my first spell had moved on.

Steve showed me a list of about 30 names. I asked him to go through them because I wanted to pick 11 players I could trust at Curzon Ashton. There was a lot of 'no's' as Steve read out the names. We struggled to get 11 worthy of the shirt as we went out of the FA Cup the following night.

My first league game at home to Chester was a big occasion for me, and the fans and the club pulled out all the stops. There was a big 'welcome home' banner behind the goal and they played the Peters and Lee song on the tannoy. The game itself went well until the 90th minute when Chester scraped an equaliser.

Getting that all-important first win then proved elusive as I found out more about my new team. The dressing room was the worst of all worlds – too big, and lacking quality in ability and character. We were hit by injuries and plagued by excuses. The dressing room can make or break a manager and I had a poor one.

I knew I needed 'proper men' to give us a chance of beating relegation. Dan Parslow came back on loan from Cheltenham; I signed left back Sean Newton, from Wrexham, and rediscovered Vadaine Oliver, who had been on loan at Notts County. I was told the striker was difficult to handle but decided to make up my own mind and he did well for us.

Vadaine combined up front with Amari Morgan-Smith, and a blast from York's past in Jon Parkin. 'The beast', as he was known, was a big man with a big heart. I got him at the end of his career and had to manage him carefully. There was no point insisting he trained every day when his body wouldn't take it, so I gave him time off when he needed it. I also asked him on an away trip what he liked to do on a Friday night. "Drink six pints!" he replied. "Ok, have your six pints, as long as you're ready for 3pm tomorrow," I said.

We finally broke our duck at North Ferriby on Boxing Day after 11 games. By now, we were in deep relegation trouble, but the club generally was in a more positive state. I had a good, experienced dressing room to work with, but that had taken time.

We were a top six side from then on. We won eight and drew eight of our 21 games, hardly relegation form. Throw in our second brilliant FA Trophy triumph and that was five losses in 26.

But, when you are near the bottom, it's very difficult to get out. Best we could do was close the gap on the clubs above us rather than pull clear of the bottom four.

Beating Lincoln City, flying high at the top of the Conference, in the semi final of the Trophy showed how good and confident we were. Leading 2-1 from the first leg, Scott Fenwick's penalty edged us through at Sincil Bank after they scored first.

Another trip to Wembley was exciting, but there was no time to dwell on it. We still had a lot of league games to play and the last thing I wanted was to go into the Trophy final with a relegated team.

The stats show we did well in our last 10 matches, winning five and drawing two. A 2-0 victory at Chester took us out of the bottom four for the first time in several months. Then three more points at Solihull Moors boosted our prospects still further with three games left.

We couldn't afford a slip up and that came when my old club Wrexham won 3-1 at Bootham Crescent. That sent us to fellow strugglers Woking back in the relegation zone. A 1-1 draw meant our fate wasn't in our own hands going into the final game at home to Forest Green Rovers.

We needed to better Guiseley's result at home to Solihull. I told our players to do their jobs and go for the victory to give us the best possible chance. Forest Green was an odd one. The aristocrats of Non-League, they were assured of their play off spot with only pride to play for. At half time we were trailing 2-1, but Guiseley were losing too.

Our position changed when Jon Parkin scored his second goal of the game to haul us back to 2-2. With minutes ticking away and Guiseley still losing, we were heading for safety. Then disaster struck. Rovers boss Mark Cooper had just whispered in my ear we were nearly safe when news came through of Guiseley's late equaliser.

I got the message to our players that we needed a goal. There were only a couple of minutes left and we had one chance. At the final whistle, silence descended on Bootham Crescent. You could hear a pin drop. The horrible eerie feeling that we had been relegated begun to sink in.

Shaking people's hands, clapping the fans, speaking to the press – all killed me. They were among the hardest things I have ever done as a manager. But I had to be professional. I still had a football club to run with a Wembley final in three weeks.

I was alone in my office when the chairman and club secretary Lisa walked in. He handed me an envelope saying I should read the letter when I got home and tell him my answer the next day. What? I wanted to know what was in it there and then! What a moment to confront me when I was at my very lowest.

Jason told me there were conditions in there for me to stay on as manager. These included having to ask permission from Jackie McNamara if I wanted to give players a day off. My authority as manager was being taken away.

I read the letter in full with Sue, Cask, and his wife Victoria, back at the apartment. It was appalling and the timing even worse. I asked Jason if I had to agree to these conditions to lead my team out at Wembley. He said that was correct.

With such a long time until the final and having suffered a devastating blow, I gave the players 10 days off. No doubt some people would argue that they hadn't earned the break after being relegated, but that's not the point. I wanted them to get away from the press and the negativity, and instead clear their minds for the challenge ahead. In my view, that's part of a manager's job.

Sue and I went on holiday to Crete. On day two, Jackie McNamara rang to ask what I had decided. I told him I had handed the letter on to the League Managers Association to get their advice. Their response was that I couldn't agree to any of it, and they had never seen conditions like them before.

When I got back from holiday, I sat down with the chairman and agreed a salary. There was no talk about any of the clauses from the letter in my new contract. Instead, I was left to prepare my team for Wembley.

We then had a good week on the training pitch to focus our minds on the Trophy final. I wasn't approaching the game as the last of the season after being relegated, but as a new start. In any case, any game at Wembley is a big occasion, and Cask and I were determined to do all we could to put a smile on the faces of our fans who had been through so much - good and bad – over the past 10 years.

It says so much that, although they were still suffering from the shock of going down, the supporters turned out in their thousands for what turned out to be a close and exciting game.

Jon Parkin's opening goal felt special to me. It was almost as if I had scored myself. Here he was, almost at the end of his career, getting a chance to play at the national stadium and putting his name on the scoresheet. I couldn't have been more pleased that it was him who set us on the way. I likened it to when Jack Lester scored for Gateshead at Wembley in his final professional game. But thankfully, this time Jon was on the winning side.

Macclesfield equalised later in the first half before Vadaine Oliver edged us back in front at 2-1. I was almost walking down the tunnel preparing my team talk for the second half when we conceded a second leveller right on half time. That always changes what a manager is planning to say, but I did my best to lift the players again.

Macclesfield had their share of chances, but the winning goal went our way. Jon Parkin was again heavily involved – that's not a pun. His shot from the edge of the box was deflected and bound for the net when up popped substitute Aidan Connolly to make sure.

I felt great at the final whistle. It was another proud moment, the third time I had won at Wembley as York manager. And I could see the elation on the faces of our supporters.

That inevitably was the last time several of those players put on a York City shirt. There's always plenty of chopping and changing at the end of a season and having to prepare a team for Conference North made it more difficult.

I sat down with players such as Jon Parkin, Dan Parslow, and others, who had played much higher in their careers and was delighted when they all agreed to play for me. That loyalty highlighted the relationship I had with the players with the majority wanting to help me try to take York City back up.

We were in the top six and had beaten Salford City in the FA Cup when I got the sack after 12 league games. We hadn't adjusted perfectly to our new league but were up there with a chance. Things started to turn with a defeat at Harrogate where I took a lot of abuse from fans, including one who spat at me. Then, the following week, we went out of the Cup to a last-minute goal by a South Shields side, including two or three of my Gateshead players.

I was driving back to Nottingham when Jason McGill phoned to tell me it was the end of the road for me. You learn sometimes from bitter experiences how things are done in football, but that wasn't a very professional way of handling a sensitive issue. The very least I would have expected was being told face to face.

I found out why the chairman had been so hasty the next morning when I looked on the club website and a new manager was already in place. That was a very sad end to the relationship I had with Jason McGill that started so well when I first joined York, but it had long since become very distant. I have thought long and hard about why the chairman reappointed me. Perhaps he did it to get the fans off his back; perhaps he thought I could recreate the magic of my first spell. I nearly did. I have to say that my second departure from York felt personal.

Getting the sack meant I had time to have my hip replacement. I'd been in a lot of pain and it had become a standing joke in training when the ball came towards me and I collapsed. "Gaffer's down!" they cried. I blamed Cask! The hip was already bad but got worse when we used to play tennis at Wrexham. I swear his drop shots were the final straw!

Sue and others encouraged me to take time away from football management but, in all honesty, I would have delayed the operation had I landed another job. I got down to the last two at Solihull Moors, who opted instead for Mark Yates, and had an interview at Halifax.

Undergoing the surgery realistically put me out of the frame for a football job for about six months, and instead I started working with my brothers Martyn and Graham for the family firm Mills Carpentry and Building Services, which I've continued to do over the last couple of years.

I'm very proud of both of them and was more than happy to work for them. Working in the building trade has been something new and has enabled me to get to know people in a different field away from football. I enjoy good banter with folk in the building trade and they enjoy listening to my stories.

I also got to coach on the sports field where it all started through Graham, who is now the chairman of Harpole. Again, this was a surreal experience for me and one I thoroughly enjoyed. Working with a village side is not the same as being in the professional game but I applied the same principles. Those who attended my sessions knew they needed to work hard but also that I wanted them to enjoy themselves.

Of course, I was disappointed that it took such a long time to get back into football, but my next break about two years later came whilst working with my brothers. A friend called me to say that Corby Town were looking for a new manager. Corby are a Northamptonshire side, the county where my football life started, based only 30 minutes from where I was working. I applied for the job, met with chairman Steve Noble who introduced me to a very good set up, and he appointed me in August 2020 in time for what proved to be a very strange season.

Corby are currently a part time club lower in the Non-League pyramid than I'm used to. But they are ambitious, have a cracking ground with good facilities and support, and I treat the job in the same way as every other club I have managed, seeking to get the best out of the players and myself.

I may be about to celebrate my 60th birthday but I'm still a Young Millsy at heart and my ambitions haven't changed – I still want to manage as high as I possibly can. Corby kindly have given me the chance to try to take them to a higher level, and things went well in the first few months for me and Geebo, who has again become my assistant. We got ourselves to the top of the league after seven games before the lockdowns and the coronavirus ended our season.

Nobody knows what is around the corner in football but, at the time of writing, I'm turning my attention to putting together a side for the 2021/22 season, with the same enthusiasm and excitement as when I set out on my managerial career all those years ago at Grantham Town.

CHAPTER 14
GREAT EXPECTATIONS AND TRUE SUCCESS

By SUE MILLS

PEOPLE know Gary Mills as the footballer/manager, a true professional, courageous, and dedicated. I know the other side – the private, generous, humble, loyal, and loving family man to myself and our three children, Ryan, Jenna and Ria.

We've been married for 38 years and for the most part we've led a relatively normal family life. We have lived nearly all this time in the same village we live in today, giving me and the family stability and routine.

Living with a man whose life has been dominated by football is like being on a permanent rollercoaster with tremendous highs and lows. Whether it's from facing promotions, relegations, or serious injury – and we've faced all three – whatever life has thrown our way, we've gotten through it together.

Our relationship has been tested, but from the words of the great singer Gladys Knight 'I'd rather live in his world, then live without him in mine'. We've remained best friends in our time together and fortunately the good times far outweigh the bad.

Gary would give me the world if he could, as I would him. He always put me and his family first in all the decisions he's had to make.

I'm looking forward to the next chapter in our lives and here's hoping we've got another 30 years together enjoying the things we love doing.

'I love you to the moon and back'.

Sue x

*****

WHEN I go back to my first professional club, Nottingham Forest, fans often say 'you should have achieved more in the game'.

As a player, I didn't fulfil the predictions of my first gaffer Brian Clough and one of his right-hand men Alan Hill that I would play for England at full senior level. As a manager, I set my sights at the highest level but have spent most of my 23 years in charge of non-League clubs, including several in the Conference (now National) League.

But I don't feel any sense of failure or lack of fulfilment. Of course, had I three wishes, I would have used two to play for my country at senior level and manage a side as successful as Brian Clough's. But I'm more than happy to swap both for the wonderful memories I have from a lifetime in the sport I love.

When players or managers achieve success, such as titles and trophies, they set the bar very high. Their very difficult task, in the words of my old gaffer in his famous interview with his rival Don Revie, is then to 'win better'. Anything less is viewed by the critics and some fans as failure.

My personal expectations after going into professional football as a 'Young Millsy' were set sky high. I made my First Division debut at 16 years old; was involved in two European Cup winning sides by 18 and, appeared in a Soccer Bowl final aged 20.

Forest fans look back on what happened in the years after our incredible triumphs and miss the point. Of course, it's true the teams I played in before I left the City Ground in 1987 never reached the same heights. But consistently being in the top half of the First Division and going close to winning the UEFA Cup is real success by Forest's standards. It's certainly not failure.

And I don't make excuses about my own career. I could, if I wished, look back on the serious leg break I suffered in America and claim that hampered my career. It was an horrific incident I wouldn't wish on anyone. Did it take the edge off the lightning pace I had as a teenager? I don't believe so. Rather than holding me back, that setback motivated and inspired me. I dug deep and was determined to show the football world what Gary Mills is all about – and I believe I did just that.

And neither was leaving Forest and the First Division a backward step. It's true that had I signed my three-year contract and stayed, I could have been part of the Gaffer's talented young side that won more trophies a couple of years on. But moving on was part of me growing up as a young man. Standing up for my principles and to Brian Clough, which as you can imagine was a particularly hard thing to do, was more important for me as a footballer and a person.

During my time at Forest, I'd done as I was told. The move to America wasn't my idea – but I went along with it and had a great time until my injury. I never dreamt of playing for Forest's main rivals Derby County, but I did so and am proud of representing another top East Midlands club. Then I got pushed around when I returned from America having to go to the PFA to get paid. All that time, I wanted my European Cup medal and to play regularly in the Gaffer's side. Then, when I felt I was producing my best football for Forest, I was offered a deal that didn't do me justice. The money didn't matter, but I needed to feel valued. And the missing medal was a symbol of that.

That's when I became a stronger man and started making my own decisions. People might think I was crazy joining Notts two divisions below, but I put myself into good hands. I was playing alongside my friends Garry Birtles and Paul Hart, and Alan Hill was on the staff. I also knew they had a good manager in John Barnwell, a man who was to have a big influence on my life. Ok, it didn't work out as I expected. But part of my football heart now belongs at Meadow Lane after two playing spells and my short reign as manager. Notts County Football Club means a lot to me.

It was through Notts that I discovered Leicester City. Wow, what an incredible time I had at Filbert Street. I look at what The Foxes have achieved since with a whole lot of pride. If any club can claim to have come close to matching Forest's achievements against all odds, it is now Leicester City, particularly after their Premier League win. The five years I had there were a pure rollercoaster. There were desperate lows before that final high of gaining promotion to the topflight at Wembley.

Even though it was in the Championship, it was at Leicester where I probably played my best football. As at Forest, I was part of a fantastic team spirit, that is what this wonderful game is all about. I met and played with people who have become friends for life. Then I had that great last honour of leading my team out against Derby County. So, yes, I'm a Leicester City man as well!

Then I had the experience of going back to Notts and playing for Howard Kendall. Speaking with a great manager going through hard times when he invited me into his office for a beer – or two – was a treasure I will never forget. And perhaps, too, it taught me a lesson for my own career in management – you can do all the right things, methods that have brought success in the past, and sometimes it just doesn't happen. That's football.

Ask most former footballers and they'll tell you there's no way you can replace the joy of playing the game. I was thrilled that after starting my professional career so young, I was still playing at a good level until my late 40s.

Looking back, about half-a-dozen managers influenced me in different ways. I thank them all for showing me how things should be done – and, on occasions, how they shouldn't.

But the important thing is that I have always been myself. I haven't set out to be another Brian Clough, John Barnwell, or Howard Kendall. I have stayed true to my methods and principles and the results I have got have come doing it my way.

Inevitably, the strongest influence was Brian Clough, both because he was my first professional manager and his brilliance. I have told you here only a fraction of my rollercoaster experience playing for a football genius. I have chosen to keep the rest to myself. But, despite the disappointing way it ended, nothing can buy the incredible times I enjoyed at the City Ground.

Fans laugh at some stories told at question-and-answer sessions. Ok, I know the tales of some are exaggerated but, hand on heart, what I have written about is true. Brian Clough's methods were so 'out there', people can be forgiven for thinking he was lucky for what he achieved. I know, from personal experience, that wasn't so.

The apparent 'madness' of Brian Clough was, in my view, high intelligence. I've already used the word 'genius'. His self-confidence, arrogance, if you prefer, rubbed off on us. He had the personality and charisma, backed by what he had already achieved at Derby County, to gain our total trust in what he was doing. Footballers often don't know how good they are or can be. Forest's players were convinced we were even better than we were, if that's possible.

The way he relaxed us physically and mentally was brilliant. Modern day managers could learn so much from him. I'm not intending to criticise people I know who have different methods, but Brian Clough knew when we needed a rest rather than a tough training session. Sometimes that was the best way to bury a disappointing result and performance rather than go through the game in detail. Then, after a few days off, we came back with fresh minds and enthusiasm to tackle the next challenge.

I found the ideal mentor in Brian Clough to build on what I regard as the perfect upbringing. It was a big, big thing for a lad of 14 to train with the first team and play in the Central League, and a massive step to make my First Division debut at 16. But that happened because the biggest influences on my life were on the same page. I was brought up as a youngster with the discipline to do the right things and make the most of my talent. When I went to Forest, Brian Clough and his staff recognised that and took me to a new level – but one I felt comfortable with despite my youth.

I'm incredibly proud today as a man approaching my 60th birthday of being a part of not only the greatest team in Nottingham Forest's history, but arguably the greatest achievement in the history of club football. No other club of Forest's size has even gone close to becoming European champions.

Whilst writing this book, I found myself watching TV programmes about Forest's glory days and I don't mind admitting there was more than a hint of a tear in my eye. As days and years go by, our European triumphs mean more and more to me. And, yes, I still hope one day I will get that missing medal from 1979.

Me and my Forest mates, the 'miracle men' as we are now called, played for a manager years and years ahead of his time. I honestly believe that would still be the case if he were with us in 2021.

I draw a distinction between the Gaffer's football methods and the man himself. He must be the best man manager the game has ever produced but I wouldn't recommend some of his actions as a person. Again, I am keeping some of those under my hat.

The main principle Brian Clough taught me is simplicity. Football is a simple game, it's people who make it more difficult. And Brian Clough wasn't alone in his thinking.

On my A-licence coaching course four years ago, I was with Robbie Fowler, Peter Schmeichel, Dwight Yorke, and Nigel Clough – all quality people – being instructed by Geoff Pike, who I played with at Notts County, and former Aston Villa captain Dennis Mortimer.

During a classroom discussion, we were asked what training was like when we were players. Robbie said Liverpool played eight against eight all day - just a warm-up and a practice match and no talk about the opposition. Dwight and Peter said the same. They played the same eight versus eight because they all knew their jobs. So, there was confirmation how great sides such as Liverpool and Manchester United, as well as Forest in their prime, went about their business – keeping the game simple.

That is what I mean by 'old school'. It may not get you high scores on coaching courses, but it got great results where it really matters on the pitch and I believe still does. Yes, there have been advances in the modern age we can put under the label of 'sports science', but I believe I learnt how the game should be played, and how people should be managed. And those values are not time limited.

I'll freely admit my managerial career hasn't progressed as I expected. When I told Geebo, if he joined me at Grantham, we'd go on to manage Notts County, I envisaged it being onwards and upwards from there. Perhaps it has been, but not in the traditional way people view success.

You see, it's still the same game whether you manage at Grantham Town, where I started, or Manchester United. The same but different, as Jon Parkin so rightly said. It's still a case of getting the best out of footballers to win games of football – heading and kicking to defend our box, scoring goals at the other end of the pitch. Yet we all know it's also very different – wages, crowds, and the level of media attention included.

Being 'old school' has perhaps been better suited to life further down the football pyramid.

I love having a drink and a chat with the supporters. At Forest, we walked into the Jubilee Club after matches win, lose, or draw;

there wasn't a private bar for staff and players. It was the same when we socialised in the city – fans spoke with us and we spoke to them. That's been lost in top level professional football for several reasons but lives on today in Non-League. I've also made great friends among the staff – paid officials or volunteers, whose hearts are in their clubs and would never want to be anywhere else. I keep in touch with some; some even call me 'gaffer'.

If being successful is about leaving a club in a higher position in the league than when I started, I've been successful at most clubs I've managed. The main exception was at Notts where, like Howard Kendall, the die was cast against me.

I've had more than my fair share of promotions and Wembley triumphs, complemented by near misses, and successful and unsuccessful battles against relegation. Mostly, I've been appointed by clubs needing a lift – that's the nature of the managerial game apart from for the very top – and I've never had limitless resources.

I've worked with the principles and disciplines I learnt from my life before going into management. I've gone into clubs looking to create trust between me, the players, and the rest of the staff. I've not set myself as being above or below them, everyone has their own individual job to do if we are to be successful. But I've been the one who knows he is going to stand or fall by his decisions – so I've made those decisions, however hard.

Most players I have managed will tell you they enjoyed the experience and would gladly play for me again, given the chance. The rest, those who didn't get on with me, were usually the ones who didn't take on board my ways. I don't expect ordinary mortals to be like George Best or Lionel Messi, but I expect them to be the very best that they can be.

Particularly at Non-League level, many have no idea what that means. They don't know either how good they are or what level they're capable of playing at. I give them my opinion, based on what I have learnt in the game. If they are willing to listen, work hard and improve, that's fine by me; if not, I wish them all the best in the future.

'Success' to me is about more than winning matches. I've won some of the top honours in the game, but I value the fact that I can honestly write here most people have found me worthy of trust. That, in my opinion, is as big an achievement as any title.

I've made great friends at all the clubs I've been involved with and that's another aspect of getting older. It's a pleasure, for example, to meet up again with my former teammates at Forest, usually at events organised by Mike West, who has also been one of the key people in encouraging me to do my book and make it possible.

As I was writing this, a good number of us took part in a golf day at Oakmere Golf Club in aid of Blesma which supports limbless veterans. I don't pretend to be a great golfer but seeing so many people I have shared special times with was wonderful. Then a few days later I played what will, in all probability, be my last ever football match at Basford United's ground, in aid of the Tree Tops Hospice and honouring Samantha Birtles, Garry's wife, who so sadly passed away from cancer a few days previously. I was on the pitch for barely a minute and had to hobble off with an injured achilles tendon.

Those things are reminders, perhaps, that we are all getting older and time with friends is precious. A few years ago, I had another reminder playing tennis with John Robertson at the David Lloyd Centre.

I thought nothing of it when Robbo called a sudden halt. I was used to him doing this, usually for a quick fag, with the score at 40-40. On this occasion, he started clutching his chest and saying he felt a pain. He resumed play and won the next couple of points before putting his hands on his chest again and saying he didn't feel well.

He sat down but was still suffering, so we called an ambulance. We were worried sick looking on as Robbo was sat on the table with an oxygen mask over his mouth. Suddenly he took the mask off and started to talk – I thought he was about to say something sentimental. "I won two more points even though I was having a f---ing heart attack," he said, before putting the mask back on. Bless him, Robbo, the greatest player in Forest's history, he isn't in the best of health these days, but it's always great to see him and all the others.

The lows I have had in management have prompted very important people in my life to say, 'why do you continue to do this?', or, 'isn't it time you took a break from football?' And I understand that. My wife Sue, in particular, has seen how disappointments have affected me. She knows how hard it has been for me when I have been sacked. It has genuinely hurt, and sometimes made me doubt myself.

She has been my rock in good times and bad. And I'm glad to say the former has much outnumbered the latter. Football isn't her greatest love, I know that. She has told you in this book that she made a choice to share my life and my passions and she has been with me all the way. Having a great wife and a wonderful family is also part of 'success', as I have experienced it.

And yet my loved ones know that even though their comments are logical and with my best interests at heart, football is in my blood. There's nothing I can do about it. Like a fan, who will never give up on his or her team however badly they are doing – there's always been something that has pulled me back to the game I love.

And you literally never know what is around the corner in football. One thing though I will never be is a 'manager in waiting'. Whenever I have been out of work, I have been interested in 'vacancies'. I have never been interested in a job whilst there was someone already in place. I've been approached in those circumstances once or twice and told the clubs that's not for me. Particularly at York City, a club and city where I left my heart and soul, I have experienced being sacked and a new man taking my place almost before I had driven home. That's disgraceful, in my view. I know I'm worthy of more respect than that – and that applies to most managers.

Instead, I'm very grateful that my time at the top of professional football came in better times.

Again, I'm asked if I wish I was playing in 2021 when players earn ridiculous amounts of money. And my honest answer is no. Although I live comfortably in a lovely house, I am not a rich man. But, much more importantly, I am rich in memories. And you can't put a price on them. If anything, I would have chosen to come into football even earlier than I did, perhaps in the early 1970s which was a golden era for the game.

I'm delighted to have shared my story in life and in football with you and I hope you have enjoyed reading it.

But this is far from the final whistle. I still have that burning desire to be the best – to win and win more. My body may be telling me another story right now, but my mind is still that of a Young Millsy bursting to show the world what I can do.

Gary Mills

A MESSAGE FROM THE GHOSTWRITER

GARY asked me to write a piece which I'm delighted to do.

It's a long time since 'Gary who?' became a part of my life as a teenage football fan. I was in the middle of the Trent End, more than a little perplexed when the names of Gary Mills and Garry Birtles were read out before Forest's First Division game against Arsenal.

Less than two years later, both young men were running their hearts out in Madrid as Forest rounded off the most amazing three years in club football with their second European Cup win.

Much later, I did two or three interviews with Gary for the Non-League Paper. What struck me, then, was what a particularly polite and down-to-earth guy he was.

Working with Gary on his book has been amazing. I've met a few people in life who have told me 'What you see is what you get', and that's been far from the case. Gary Mills is the person football fans perceive him to be from his always hard working, disciplined, and talented performances on the field.

Although I will always regard him as a Forest man, supporters of many clubs throughout the country, and in Seattle, have great affection for him. I hope I've helped him do justice to show what he means to all of them.

I sincerely wish to thank Mike West for inviting me to speak with Gary, the sponsors of this book Richard Waring and Superstar Speakers, and my colleagues Barrie Pierpoint and Mathew Mann for their practical support in making Young Millsy happen.

Meeting your heroes and finding them worthy of that support is a lovely experience. I'm more pleased than ever I turned up now to watch Gary Mills that unforgettable Saturday – as a certain someone would have said, 'he is a credit to his profession'.

John Brindley

Playing Statistics

	Appearances	Goals
Nottingham Forest 1978 - 1982	77	10
Seattle Sounders 1982 - 1983	34	5
Derby County 1982 - 1983	23	2
Nottingham Forest 1983 - 1987	96	5
Notts County 1987 - 1989	96	9
Leicester City 1989 - 1994	232	16
Notts County 1994 - 1996	63	0
Grantham Town 1996 - 1998	96	3
Gresley Rovers 1998	7	0
King's Lynn 1998 - 2000	80	3
Boston United 2000 - 2001	8	0
Tamworth 2001 - 2002	46	2
Alfreton Town 2005 - 2007	26	0
Tamworth 2007 - 2010	14	0
England (Under-18) 1978 - 1979	2	0
England (Under-21) 1981	2	0
Total	**902**	**55**

Managerial Statistics

	Games	Won	Draw	Lost	Win %
Grantham Town 1996 - 1998	111	65	17	29	58.6
King's Lynn 1998 - 2000	106	45	30	31	42.5
Tamworth 2001 - 2002	71	40	20	11	56.3
Notts County 2004	40	10	11	19	25.0
Alfreton Town 2005 - 2007	76	21	27	28	27.6
Tamworth 2007 - 2010	189	75	50	64	39.7
York City 2010 - 2013	136	58	45	33	42.6
Gateshead 2013 - 2015	103	46	32	25	44.7
Wrexham 2015 - 2016	64	26	13	25	40.6
York City 2016 - 2017	53	20	17	16	37.7
Total	**949**	**406**	**262**	**281**	**42.7**

Honours

AS PLAYER

European Cup Nottingham Forest	Winner	1979, 1980
European Super Cup Nottingham Forest	Winner Runners Up	1979 1980
Division One - Play-Off Leicester City	Runners Up Winner	1992, 1993 1994
Anglo-Italian Cup Notts County	Winners	1995
Division Two - Play-Off Notts County	Runners Up	1996

AS MANAGER

Southern Football League Grantham Town	Champions	1998
Conference North Tamworth	Champions	2009
Conference Premier Play-Off York City	Winners	2012
FA Trophy York City	Winners	2012, 2017
Conference Play-Off Gateshead	Runners Up	2014

**Wembley visits 10, six as player and four as manager.
Overall six wins, four losses.**

Played eight times for England Schoolboys, scoring one goal.

MORGAN LAWRENCE
P U B L I S H I N G   S E R V I C E S

The following books are also available to purchase from
morganlawrence.co.uk and all major book retailers

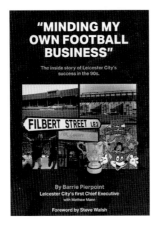

Minding My Own Football Business
By Barrie Pierpoint

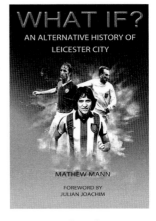

What If?
By Mathew Mann

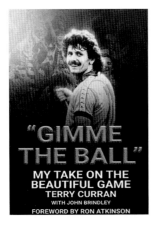

Gimme The Ball
By Terry Curran

You Must Be Joachim
By Julian Joachim

Email: hello@morganlawrence.co.uk
Telephone: 07514 116 493